INDUSTRAT: The Strategic Industrial Marketing Simulation

Jean-Claude Larréché and David Weinstein

INSEAD
Fontainebleau

Prentice Hall, Englewood Cliffs, New Jersey 07632

Library of Congress Cataloging-in-Publication Data

Larreche, Jean-Claude
    INDUSTRAT : The strategic industrial marketing
simulation

    Includes index
    1 Industrial marketing   2 Management games.
I Weinstein, David, (date).   II Title
HF5415 1263 L37 1987   658.8   87-7144
ISBN 0-13-459157-7

Editorial/production supervision
    and interior design: **Cheryl Lynn Smith**
Cover design: **Wanda Lubelska**
Manufacturing buyer: **Barbara Kittle**

© 1988 by Jean-Claude Larréché and David Weinstein

Printed in the United States of America

10

ISBN 0-13-459157-7 01

Prentice-Hall International (UK) Limited, *London*
Prentice-Hall of Australia Pty. Limited, *Sydney*
Prentice-Hall Canada Inc., *Toronto*
Prentice-Hall Hispanoamericana, S.A., *Mexico*
Prentice-Hall of India Private Limited, *New Delhi*
Prentice-Hall of Japan, Inc., *Tokyo*
Simon & Schuster Asia Pte. Ltd., *Singapore*
Editora Prentice-Hall do Brasil, Ltda., *Rio de Janeiro*

SOFTWARE ORDERING INFORMATION

Prices are valid for the 1987–1988 academic year. Payment is made on a usage basis, the fee applying to each individual run of an industry consisting of five teams.

- For executive development seminars or commercial executive training companies . . . $5,000 U.S. dollars
- For public executive development seminars run within academic institutions and regarded as semi-commercial operations . . . $1,500 U.S. dollars
- In an MBA program . . . $150 U.S. dollars

INDUSTRAT USER'S FORM

INDUSTRAT: The Industrial Marketing Simulation will be used by myself under the following circumstances:

Course Date _____

Course Name _____

Program (check one)   MBA _____   University _____   Executive _____   Private _____

Number of Participants _____

Number of Industries _____

Desired Delivery Date _____

Delivery Address _____

_____

_____

Telephone _____

Telex _____

Invoice Address (if different) _____

Name _____

Signature/Date _____

All software should be ordered through David Weinstein, not Prentice Hall.

Professor David Weinstein
INSEAD
Bld de Constance
77305 Fontainebleau Cedex
France
Phone: (1) 60 72 42 00
Telex: 690389

Contents

Preface

Development of this simulation was motivated by our desire to improve the traditional approach to industrial marketing education. Training and educational efforts in this important area have traditionally relied on lectures and case discussions supplemented by assigned readings and exercises. These tools represent the best that pedagogical technology has been able to offer. However, the modern competitive industrial environment requires a new pedagogical approach.

Consider pilots, fire fighters, and cardiologists, three professions requiring skillful decision-making under pressure. The heavy cost of erring in such occupations makes training through first hand experience crucial. The competitiveness of the industrial environment has intensified to a point where the costliness of faulty marketing decisions justifies such analogies. Companies that could afford certain mistakes in the past would not recover from the adverse effects of those very errors today.

The success of many industrial firms may initially be attributed to their products and technological advantages. Once competitors develop similar products the technological edge tends to diminish. The market then fragments and the concept of competitive advantage and the vision guiding it must change.

Numerous publications and speeches have noted the importance of strategic market orientation in today's environment. They all conclude that one can no longer afford to make mistakes. Market orientation implies allocating resources to research and development which will yield products with a sustainable advantage, while current products and technologies, based on past strategies, compete and survive. This requires careful identification and definition of markets coupled with anticipation of competitors' behavior. It also implies an understanding of customers' behavior and their responses to the different marketing tools available in the short run.

Training in strategic marketing, which allows an easy transition from the classroom to the field, has become invaluable. Computerized simulations of actual operating environments have proven effective in the many areas which require the building of skills before actual application is called for. In industrial marketing this method should place managers in the midst of a competitive scenario and provide them with instant feedback to their decisions. The pedagogical objectives of such an exercise are to

1. provide direct experience with the concepts and processes of strategic marketing,
2. integrate, in an operational way, concepts learned through other educational vehicles, and
3. experiment with new competitive scenarios.

The INDUSTRAT simulation provides a live experience in management where teams must bear the consequences of their own decisions. The pressure of this setting brings out enthusiasm and a competitive spirit, which create an enjoyable learning experience.

This simulation follows MARKSTRAT[1], the design that marked the beginning of a generation of realistic and strategy-oriented simulations. MARKSTRAT offers the following features:

1. Simulated periods of one year each, making long range planning possible and allowing evaluation of strategies in retrospect.
2. Emphasis on segmentation as a basis for marketing strategy.
3. Emphasis on positioning issues in the formulation of marketing strategies. Participants formulate and execute marketing strategies using recently developed positioning analysis techniques and graphics.
4. Possibilities to manage a product line through modification of existing products and the introduction of new ones. Thus, marketing resources are allocated across a portfolio of products/markets.
5. Interaction between marketing and R&D to develop products with specific physical characteristics.
6. Clear distinction, supported by marketing research data, between the physical characteristics of products and their perception by customers.
7. Extensive set of market research studies, representing modern methodological and conceptual developments in industrial marketing thought.
8. Dynamic environment containing competitive moves, emerging product categories, productivity gains through experience effects, and a changing economic environment.
9. Realistic environment where each firm has its own inherent strengths and weaknesses in brand awareness, technology, distribution, and profitability.
10. Simulated marketing phenomena which are sufficiently intricate and diverse for participants to adopt a *learning* rather than a *gaming* behavior.

MARKSTRAT is based on a durable consumer goods scenario. It goes a long way to effectively train managers for strategic marketing. The record of adoption by universities and corporations and the feedback from numerous seminars designed around this tool are testimony to the impact of this simulation on marketing education. However, for a deeper and more advanced treatment of industrial marketing strategy, the particular context of the simulated markets becomes more important.

The difference between consumer and industrial marketing environments implies obvious differences in the respective marketing mixes with respect to pricing methods, communication tools, distribution channels, and product management. Moreover, the

---

[1] Jean-Claude Larréché and Hubert Gatignon, *MARKSTRAT. A Marketing Strategy Game*, (Palo Alto, CA: The Scientific Press, 1977).

complexity of the industrial market environment entails differences in market analysis. That is why we embarked on the development of INDUSTRAT.

The INDUSTRAT simulation is designed to train marketers in strategy making skills while working in a simulated, yet realistic, industrial environment. More specifically, while containing the features described previously, this simulation incrementally offers:

1. Industrial target accounts containing several decision makers, each with his or her own favorite suppliers' concerns, biases, and relative influence at different instances.

2. Separation of market segmentation into macrosegmentation and microsegmentation issues. The former is based on characteristics of accounts and the latter on characteristics of decision-makers within the accounts.

3. Customer accounts with decision makers who, as industrial customers, are concerned with multi-sourcing issues.

4. Evolution of the status of suppliers from *testing* through *supplementary source* to *primary source*.

5. Separation of corporate positioning of the supplying establishment from the positioning of the physical product it sells.

6. Separation of the R&D function into basic technological research and product development activities.

7. Possibility for collaboration between competing companies through licensing agreements.

8. Detailed management of the sales force and technical support organizations via employment, hiring, firing, alternative organizations, guiding, and training.

9. Detailed treatment of other industrial marketing mix decisions including list prices, price discounts, sales commission, sales force, promotion, product advertising, and corporate advertising.

10. Provision of a comprehensive set of customer based market research studies specifically designed for industrial products.

INDUSTRAT was designed as an integrating vehicle to be used in conjunction with other pedagogical tools. The simulation should ordinarily be supplemented by case discussions and lectures, introducing strategic notions and techniques, and illustrating actual application areas. The target audience for INDUSTRAT is composed of participants in advanced industrial marketing strategy courses.

The INDUSTRAT simulation enjoyed the programming talents of Elspeth Fleming, Edward Heath and Viviane Tetard, who, with tenacity and good humour, enabled us to traverse the rough terrain which a project of this magnitude had in store. This effort was further enhanced by the professional and enthusiastic support of our friends, Paule Villain and Pierre-Yves Saint Oyant, at INSEAD's computer center. We are particularly grateful to Sarah Lea-Wilson for her contribution to INDUSTRAT in editing and word processing and in the preparation of other documentation. Lynn Gray and Catherine Penou have also contributed greatly at various stages of the development and the testing of the simulation.

Special thanks and acknowledgment go to a large industrial marketing company which served as an inspiration and provided information for the context which we simulated. Senior executives in this firm submitted themselves to the initial running of the simulation and provided valuable feedback. The first program to include the INDUSTRAT simulation was the Advanced Industrial Marketing Strategy seminar which took place at INSEAD in June 1984. We would like to thank the executives from various corporations who attended this seminar and whose enthusiastic feedback provided the quality stamp of approval required before opening this simulation to a wider audience.

The development of INDUSTRAT was sponsored by INSEAD, the European Institute of Business Administration, and by CEDEP, the European Centre for Continuing Education, both in Fontainebleau, France. We acknowledge the financial assistance of both institutions and the moral support of our colleagues throughout the project.

In such developments the most important thanks should go to the families on the sidelines. Our families carried the brunt of the load and provided powerful encouragement—to them we dedicate INDUSTRAT.

Jean-Claude Larréché and David Weinstein

INSEAD
Fontainebleau

chapter I

Introduction

Three skills are necessary for strategic marketing decisions: analysis, recognition of concepts, and decision-making under uncertainty. The first two skills are crucial since many variables operate simultaneously in a competitive market. A simulation of an industrial market will help managers to reinforce their business judgement, sharpen their analysis and improve their sensitivity to market signals. Since uncertainties are always inherent in markets and many of the variables are beyond the marketer's control, the total removal of risk is impossible—even following exhaustive analysis. However, simulating a market teaches managers how to determine whether certain events are likely to occur and make the best possible decision, despite the presence of uncertainty. This chapter discusses strategy formulation and execution in an industrial marketing context—the area (see Figure 1-1) where these skills are so necessary and for which INDUSTRAT was designed—and then describes the simulation itself and the learning experience it will provide.

THE INDUSTRIAL MARKETING CONTEXT

In all marketing situations one finds, on the one hand, consumers with certain needs and, on the other, suppliers competing to satisfy these needs at a profit. It is generally agreed that in spite of differences between sectors, strategic concepts like market segmentation and positioning are universally applicable. Yet, in general, industrial marketers tend to lag behind their counterparts in the consumer goods sector in the use of strategic concepts.

The reason for the lag lies mainly in the circumstances that make industrial marketing unique. Industrial purchasing is usually performed by a group of individuals on behalf of an organization. The needs of industrial purchasers differ greatly from those of consumer goods purchasers, as do the processes they follow in making a purchase and the settings in which they operate. Let us briefly discuss these general differences in order to set the scene for the INDUSTRAT simulation.

The demand for an industrial product or service is derived from the demand for

REVIEW OF STRATEGIC CONCEPTS	APPLICATION IN AN INDUSTRIAL MARKETING CONTEXT	FOCUS ON PRIME INDUSTRIAL MARKETING ISSUES
• MARKET SEGMENTATION • POSITIONING/REPOSITIONING • PORTFOLIO APPROACH • THE MARKETING PLAN	• ORGANIZATIONS AS TARGETS • MACROSEGMENTS AND MICROSEGMENTS • CUSTOMER - SUPPLIER RELATIONSHIPS • THE INDUSTRIAL MARKETING MIX	• CUSTOMER PRODUCT/NON PRODUCT NEEDS • CUSTOMER DECISION MAKING PROCESS • SALES AND TECHNICAL ORGANIZATIONS • DISTINCTION BETWEEN RESEARCH & DEVELOPMENT • COMPETITION AND COLLABORATION

Figure 1-1 Objectives of INDUSTRAT.

yet another product or service. The buying organization involves several individuals in the purchasing process, who act and interact according to their individual responsibilities, their firm's needs, the distribution of power, and group dynamics. Some of the considerations these persons take into account are professional and rational; other considerations may not directly relate to their task but may be more personal in nature. Each participant in the purchasing process may perceive the value of a competitive supplier's products, services, and relationship differently.

An industrial product, once supplied, enters a production process which is often costly and risky to change. This gives the current industrial supplier a certain stability that other competitors must overcome. For example, a manufacturer of automobiles, whose product has been competing successfully, would hesitate to replace a proven supplier of sensitive components with an untried one. Similarly, an organization may elect to retain a second-best computer system for fear of conversion costs.

The exchange between an industrial supplier and a customer involves more than just the physical product. A supplier may offer a superior product, yet may not have success with a customer because of other factors, such as service and support. Examples of such situations abound in technology-based industries. Often, technically superior products fail because suppliers fail to provide the technical support customers require.

Transactions in industrial markets usually involve large financial commitments and organizational risks for the customer. Both customers and suppliers tend to have risk-reducing mechanisms—some formally designed and others developed through personal relationships—which lead to a diversification in purchasing and sales. Such processes strengthen the bonds between the two parties, which has an impact on the speed with which a relationship may realistically be expected to change.

Another significant feature of industrial marketing is the concentration of the market. It is not unusual to find a competitive arena with few suppliers and few customer companies. This concentration has an impact on personal relationships and competitive practices in the market.

The complexity of products and buyer-supplier relationships in an industrial market means that management of the human element is crucial in industrial marketing. People communicate with customers and transmit their feedback to the firm; people also perform technical support activities. As a result, personnel management—including hiring, organizing, motivating and firing of people—is of unique importance to industrial marketing.

Parts of the industrial sector rely heavily on research and development. Since R&D is usually costly and time consuming, and since customers prefer more than one source of supply, it is not unusual to see competitors collaborate in licensing agreements and joint ventures.

All of these distinctive features of industrial marketing are found in INDUSTRAT, as they have an impact both on the strategy formulation and execution stages of the management process. Industrial marketers should feel quite at home with the INDUS-TRAT environment. The simulation is a result of observing various industrial marketing scenarios. It is fairly complex, yet well structured to provide an effective learning environment.

INDUSTRIAL MARKETING STRATEGY

Marketing strategy is the set of choices made by a firm in allocating its scarce resources as it competes with other firms to satisfy customers' needs. Typically, resources are allocated with respect to products, geographical territories, or other strategic business units. The manner in which resources are allocated depends on the answers to the following five questions:

1. How should the market be broken down into segments?
2. Which segments constitute targets?
3. What proportion of the available resources should be allocated to each segment?
4. Which customers' needs should be satisfied?
5. How can competitive advantage be sustained, or built, over time?

Making these decisions in an industrial marketing environment is a complex task. By integrating major features of industrial markets into the making of strategy, the INDUSTRAT simulation provides managers with a realistic exercise in decision-making.

THE INDUSTRIAL MARKETING MIX

The formulation of an industrial marketing strategy is followed by a program of execution, sometimes called the *marketing program* or *marketing mix*. The marketing program specifies the various activities involved in executing the strategy including communication, pricing, sales force, and product management. Although production, R&D, and, in many cases, the sales force are not usually within the jurisdiction of the marketing department, their activities must be carried out in harmony with the marketing plan.

The formulation of the industrial marketing mix requires an understanding of the client company's purchasing behavior, the individuals involved, and their interactions. Once a marketing plan is formulated, the various activities in the plan are translated into a budget, which is evaluated in light of the income it will generate for the company. Once this evaluation is made, there may be a need to make changes in the marketing mix. Further changes may be required even at the strategic levels, as obstacles may arise during the execution of the plan.

THE INDUSTRAT COMPETITIVE SCENARIO: AN OVERVIEW

INDUSTRAT is a simulation of six to ten years of competition among five firms which currently produce, promote, and sell a product called *Korex*. Korex is used in the manufacture of products for industrial, as well as consumer use. The five firms have been selling Korex for some time. Industry observers feel that some of the firms might be able to develop another product, *Lomex*, using new technology. Lomex would also be used in the manufacture of both industrial and consumer products. If Lomex does appear on the market, it will not compete with Korex because their applications are unrelated. However, within the firms the two products may compete for resources, which could indirectly affect their respective markets.

Each firm starts the simulation with inherent strengths and weaknesses, all relative to its competitors. Each tries to compete effectively over the duration of the simulation and to leave a strong and healthy operation at the end. INDUSTRAT is not manipulated by the simulation administrators. Instead, developments result from the actions of the five firms, and the competitive scenario in the simulation may evolve in many directions.

This encourages rigourous analysis as well as creativity on the part of the five management teams.

Every firm in INDUSTRAT faces a vast array of strategic choices. Different teams may try to execute similar strategic choices in different ways. The resulting number of competitive scenarios in this simulation is thus infinite. This flexibility, made possible by the technology of strategic marketing simulations, is invaluable to the learning which takes place throughout an INDUSTRAT simulation.

Figure 1-2 illustrates the simulation process for each *period* (representing a year in the history of the industry). Each firm receives a computer-generated report. The report is analyzed and decisions are made and submitted to the INDUSTRAT administrator. The administrator enters all the decisions into the computer and produces a report for the next *period*.

LEARNING AND INDUSTRAT

Before the simulation starts, participants should familiarize themselves with the world of INDUSTRAT, including the products, the customers, the competition, the resources under their firm's control, the administration of their company, and the paper work involved in the simulation. As each competing team will probably have just been formed, group

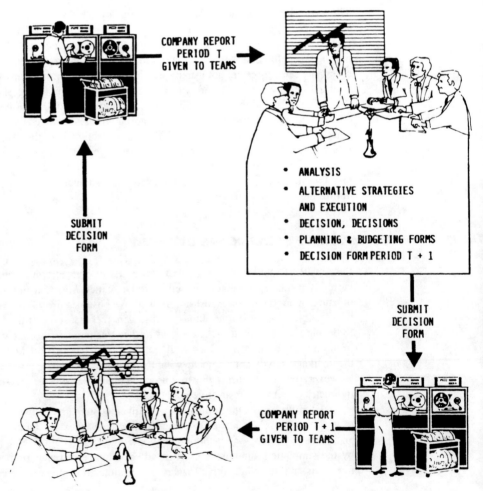

Figure 1-2   The simulation process

dynamics will not have yet evolved into a steady pattern. Since each participant will be eager and the setting competitive, the pressures will be greater than in ordinary case discussions or educational activities. Once participants have adjusted to the environment, however, conceptual learning will advance.

Although INDUSTRAT confronts the participant with a lot of information, the environment is free of much of the noise and distraction a manager usually encounters. The educational philosophy of the simulation is that once a person has used a concept or developed a skill in a controlled environment, he or she will be in a better position to apply it under more complex circumstances.

INDUSTRAT participants should be made aware of this philosophy because the actual transfer of the skills acquired in INDUSTRAT to other environments is not automatic, but must be made by the individual. Some concepts may be immediately applicable to a particular individual's situation while others prove to be less pertinent. We believe, however, that the simulation encompasses a large variety of industries and that every participant will recognize useful and practical analogies.

THIS MANUAL

This manual is designed to serve as a handbook for reference throughout the simulation. It contains administrative as well as conceptual information. Participants are not expected to memorize all the details nor comprehend all the concepts at the outset. Past experience has shown that familiarity with the INDUSTRAT environment will develop naturally as the exercise unfolds.

In preparation for the simulation participants should concentrate on those parts of the manual relating directly to the first decision. More specifically, the outgoing management of each competing firm has not left behind any market research information. Consequently, in the initial decision session, competing teams will not analyze such studies.

Similarly, participants won't make decisions about research and development nor on issues of licensing and collaboration with competitors during the first period. Participants should read the parts of this manual devoted to the aforementioned subjects only to develop an initial familiarity with the topics. Individuals will grasp certain details and concepts early on and acquire others by trading information with their teammates.

chapter 2

The INDUSTRAT Competitive Setting

Five major firms compete for Korex sales in the INDUSTRAT world. Other competitors have either left the market or are not regarded as significant enough to be of structural consequence. The events taking place in the market during the simulation will be the result of interaction among the five competitors. This chapter introduces the participant to the general economic environment and to the Korex industry and its market.

THE ECONOMIC ENVIRONMENT

The INDUSTRAT competition takes place in a major, highly developed, industrialized country (see Figure 2-1). The monetary unit in the country is the *IM* (INDUSTRAT Money, pronounced *eem*), which is represented by the symbol $. The population in this nation has reached the 250 million mark, having followed a stable annual growth rate of 1 percent per annum for the last ten years. Major economic trends in this country have been similar to those of other industrialized countries in Europe, North America, and the Far East. The country is slowly emerging from a recession which lasted over five years, and economists predict a slow but solid economic recovery. The business sector has reacted favorably to the change of economic climate and the stock markets have been bullishly boasting rising price indices.

The last three years have posted an annual real GNP growth rate of 3 percent. Inflation, which reached the 15 percent level five years ago, has been brought down slowly and is now at 10 percent per annum.

The government of the country has even supported free enterprise, regardless of the political party in power. It generally refrains from direct economic intervention and is severely criticized by opposition parties when it resorts to tools beyond the traditional fiscal and monetary means. However, there is one area in which no administration has hesitated to intervene—the protection of economic competition. Elaborate government agencies follow the evolution of industry and intervene forcefully when any collusion or

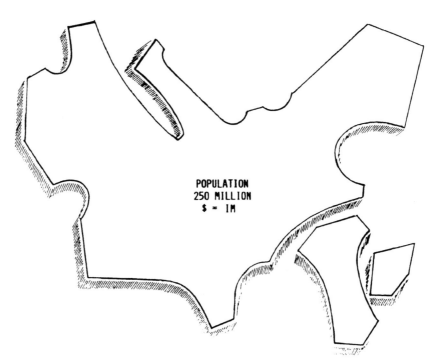

Figure 2-1 The economic environment

monopoly threat is suspected. A series of laws protect free enterprise and the sanctions for proven restriction of competition are severe. A famous recent case of collusion between competitors on prices and markets ended with senior executives serving time in prison.

The government has even intervened in some cases to keep firms from disappearing from the market in order to maintain a minimum level of competition. Recently the chairman of the board of a major firm negotiated a government guarantee for a large loan used to modernize factories and introduce a new line of products. The performance of this firm, following the controversial act, has been very promising and the value of its shares on the stock market has regained its traditionally strong level.

THE INDUSTRY

INDUSTRAT firms compete in the manufacture and marketing of industrial products based on radiochemical processes. These products serve as input for a variety of applications and industries. None of the five competing firms is forward-integrated in production, which eliminates the consideration of any internal selling. At the opening of the simulation, each firm supplies four products to its customers. Subsequently, they may introduce new products and offer a wider product line. However, each firm is limited to a maximum offering of ten products on the market at any given time.

The strategic positions of the firms differ depending on their past history. Previously, each firm followed a separate path in research and development reflecting the different assessments of the future directions of the market. The firms also differed in the way they formed and executed strategies, which influenced their effectiveness, thus leading to the relative strengths and weaknesses inherent in each firm.

The following is a description of the products marketed by the firms, the accounts, (customer organizations), the individuals involved in the accounts' purchasing decisions, and the purchasing processes themselves.

The Products

Currently the five firms compete only in the Korex market, a multipurpose, radiochemistry-based product. Although it has been on the market for almost fifteen years, use of this product was initially restricted, due to the complexity and the cost of the production process. Three years after its introduction, commercial applications started to spread as the manufacturing technology simplified. Subsequent growth rates climbed up to 40 percent six years ago. However, in the last three years the Korex market has not grown as fast. Still, since the versatility of the product has not been exhausted, overall market growth is expected to continue even though smaller manufacturers have either left the market or were absorbed by the industry leaders.

Korex comes in various physical forms according to the desired application. It may be delivered as a liquid, powder, paste, fiber, or in various solid forms. Industry experts have been quoted as saying, "Not a day passes without a new Korex application being discovered." Analysts have grouped the various areas of application into three major categories: instrumentation, communication, and consumer products. Through these categories Korex finds its way into construction, agriculture, medicine, shipbuilding, packaging, textiles, and electronics.

Each Korex product is defined by its performance characteristics. The characteristics and their respective measurement standards are

Characteristic	Measurement
1. Resistance	Ohm (Ω)
2. Suspension	Micro-second (ms)
3. Frequency	Kilo-Hertz (kHz)
4. Density	Micro-gram per cubic millimeter (mg/mm^3)

Although each physical characteristic may theoretically be specified for production, there are technological barriers to surmount before a firm may actually manufacture combinations of certain specifications. These barriers are usually overcome by research and development. Until that time, products developed by R&D only, may be manufactured.

Each INDUSTRAT firm currently produces four Korex products. The names and the actual specifications of these products are displayed in Exhibit 2-1. The first column in this exhibit shows the products currently on the market. It is easy to recognize the firm selling the product in the INDUSTRAT name convention, as illustrated in Figure 2-2. The first letter, K represents the Korex product category. The second letter, A, E, I, O, or U represents the competing firm 1, 2, 3, 4, or 5, respectively. The last two letters are freely selected by each team to designate its own products.

The next four columns display the maximum and minimum that each of the performance characteristics may take, as well as the actual values for the products present on the market at the start of the simulation. The last column in Exhibit 2-1 is the base production cost of the product as per the first 100,000 units produced, given its present production method. The firms do not have identical products on the market and, in fact, there is already some degree of specialization. As competition evolves, other Korex products will appear on the market, and some of the present ones will be modified or discontinued as firms adapt the physical characteristics of their products to the needs of the market place.

It is important to note that the perception of products may not exactly coincide with their physical specifications. Customers may, for example, perceive products as very similar within a certain range of a performance characteristic, while their actual physical measurements are significantly different. On the other hand, products which are similar

EXHIBIT 2-1

Physical Characteristics and Base Costs of Korex Models Currently Offered
on the Market

	Resistance (Ω)	Suspension (μg)	Frequency (kHz)	Density (μ/mm³)	Base costs ($)
Minimum	500	10	30	500	100
Maximum	12000	105	200	800	500
KALA	10000	50	100	750	150
KAST	1500	20	90	600	300
KAMI	6500	40	110	700	175
KAPE	1500	45	85	650	280
KENT	2000	50	90	700	250
KEPI	4000	50	95	600	300
KEEP	3000	40	130	700	300
KELY	1300	50	120	650	230
KILT	2800	100	90	600	100
KISS	3000	40	100	550	190
KIDU	6000	55	120	750	160
KINE	2800	80	110	700	150
KOPA	3500	20	115	550	250
KOLD	3000	50	130	650	300
KOPS	3000	45	120	600	300
KOOK	2000	30	120	750	280
KUST	4000	30	115	750	320
KUZZ	3500	40	115	550	300
KUTE	3000	75	80	600	250
KURE	3000	50	80	650	310

physically may be perceived as significantly different by customers. In fact, for reasons of past performance or corporate image, two physically identical products may be perceived as different.

The new product category Lomex, which may appear on the market, is based on bioengineering technology (see Figure 2-3). This product represents a basic research breakthrough by the laboratories at Stratland University, which made its research available to the industrial community. However, additional substantial investment is required for further research and development in order to manufacture the Lomex products. The industry is well positioned to develop, manufacture, and market Lomex products, which would not be competing with Korex for customers as the applications of the two are not related.

The main physical characteristics of Lomex and their respective measurements are

1. Convexity   degree (°)
2. Conductivity   micro-second (ms)
3. Purity   percentage (%)
4. Maximum Energy   micro-watt (mW)

The physical minima and maxima which each of these characteristics may take are displayed in Exhibit 2-2. As Lomex represents a new technology, the market reaction to the introduction of such products is unknown. The Lomex market may or may not develop in the way of the Korex market, depending on the rate at which new applications are developed and diffused. The naming of Lomex products will follow a similar pattern to that of Korex. The first letter, L represents Lomex and the second letter, A, E, I, O, or U identifies the firm. The remaining two will be determined by the firm's management.

Figure 2-2   The competitors

Customer Companies and Macrosegments

Because the firms in INDUSTRAT offer multipurpose versatile products, the account[1] base is extremely heterogeneous. Current and prospective accounts may differ greatly in their application of Korex, and will eventually with Lomex. In fact, they, in turn, sell their own products to a large variety of customers. This diversity poses the question of how much one should adapt products and services to satisfy the needs of individual accounts. The greater the adaptation to an individual client's needs, the more satisfied the client is likely to be. On the other hand, standardization would result in financial benefits for production economies.

To maximize the clients' satisfaction while maintaining adequate scale economies, marketers group similar customers into separate market segments. The segmentation of industrial markets may follow two levels, *macrosegments* and *microsegments*. Macrosegmentation may follow the general characteristics of the account. Microsegmentation considers the individual decision makers in the buying organizations who participate in the purchasing process; in other words, persons who occupy similar organizational positions in different customer companies.

Like many other industries, INDUSTRAT firms have developed various segmentation schemes in the face of changing market conditions. Currently, the industry uses *geographical regions, potential account size,* and *end product category* to classify client companies. The country has been divided into three territories, *eastern, central,* and *western.* Potential account sizes are grouped into *large, medium,* and *small.* The end

---

[1]For the purposes of this simulation the terms *account, client company,* and *customer company* are equivalent.

LOMEX   KOREX

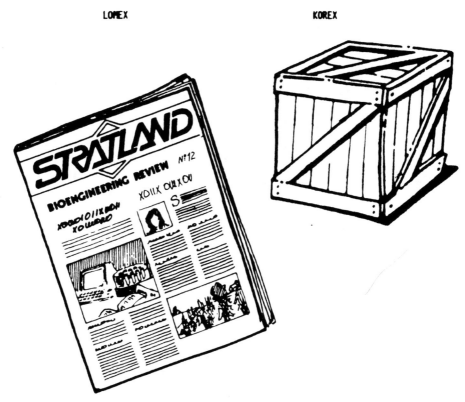

Figure 2-3 The products

product categories currently used are *instrumentation, communication,* and *consumer products.* Each account may be classified into one of the categories in each of these schemes.

The communication industry is currently the largest end-use segment in terms of Korex sales. This industry includes end products in telephone, satellite, and computerized networks. The instrumentation industry also employs varied applications of Korex for fine precision measuring instruments. Consumer products represent the remaining applications of the Korex market. This category is regarded as the least explored to date.

While the consumption of Korex has enjoyed an average annual growth of 10 percent over the last three years, industry analysts predict slower overall sales in the future. Indeed, it is only in the country's central region that sales continue to grow, while declining elsewhere. In terms of end uses, sales in the instrumentation field are expected to stabilize, while in the consumer products' category, performance has traditionally been sluggish. However, optimism has been expressed about this segment for several years. The major obstacle has been the cost of applying Korex products in comparison with

EXHIBIT 2-2

Maxima and Minima of Physical Characteristics of Lomex Products

Characteristics	Minimum	Maximum
1. Convexity (°)	5	30
2. Conductivity (μs)	50	150
3. Purity (%)	15	80
4. Maximum Energy (μW)	200	700

Note: Expected manufacturing cost per unit at the start of the simulation = $40—100.

their substitutes. Analysts agree that as the cost of production is eventually reduced, the demand for Korex will increase dramatically. As the market develops, the required investment for the usage of Korex is expected to decrease. This development may draw new client companies into the market.

Participants in the Purchasing Decision and Microsegments

Industrial customers typically follow a complex purchasing process and this industry's clients are no exception. The main reason for this complexity is the existence of the organization (tasks, responsibilities, and procedures) for purchasing. Parts of the organizational structures are formally designed and others evolve informally. The group of individuals in the purchasing process make up the *decision making unit* (DMU). Each member of the DMU contributes to the purchasing process, using his or her expertise, professional responsibilities and authority. The DMU may also include organizational procedures through which the members exchange information and resolve conflict. DMUs usually contain informal members and informal interactions which the participants use to supplement the formal process.

Two issues must be taken into account. First, the identification of the major participants of the buying center, their individual concerns, and the pattern of their interaction is crucial. Second, since the dynamics of the purchasing process vary by company, the heterogeneity of the market amplifies the variety of DMU structures with which the firms must deal.

A multiclient study sponsored by INDUSTRAT firms revealed that in spite of the diversity, customer companies do have similar profiles of the participants involved in their purchasing processes. A typical DMU is composed of four individuals, which in this industry are called production managers, engineering managers, purchasing managers, and general managers. Although formal titles vary from company to company, these terms fit the major decision makers and their counterparts in other companies who share common needs and responsibilities (see Figure 2-4).

Production managers are responsible for the manufacturing processes for Korex, and eventually for Lomex. These persons typically have one or several manufacturing plants under their control, each including several facets of production. *Engineering managers* are responsible for the technical specifications of the product. They evaluate materials, components, and production processes to fulfill the specifications required by their customers, or to achieve cost reductions. *Purchasing managers* procure alternative sources and continuity of supply, and minimize the purchasing costs. At the top, *general managers* have the overall responsibility for the performance of their companies, and their preoccupations span marketing, production, finance, R&D, personnel, and other managerial functions.

The Purchasing Process

The existence of the various accounts and persons involved in each purchasing decision implies a diversity of purchasing processes. The interaction between persons and the variety of group dynamics and management styles makes every account's purchasing process unique. This diversity poses a managerial choice as to the extent to which the structure of an account is considered in the execution of strategies. At one extreme, managers may try to become intimately aware of each individual account, each relationship, and the behavior of the people in question. On the other extreme, management may disregard its accounts' various purchasing processes and rely instead on sales personnel and others who are in touch with the individual customers to handle the relationship.

The actual choice is generally made through market segmentation, which assumes typical profiles of accounts representing each segment. An understanding of the typical

Figure 2-4   The decision making unit

account purchasing process has evolved over the years, resulting in a systematic framework which is generally applicable to accounts in this industry. It does not represent any single company in complete detail, yet captures enough of what actually takes place in many cases. This framework is managerially meaningful to the firms competing in INDUS-TRAT. It divides the purchasing decision into the chronological stages of the adoption process that a product must undergo to become a primary source of supply.

Four stages have been identified: awareness, testing, supplementary source of supply, and primary source of supply (see Figure 2-5). *Awareness*, in the industrial marketing sense, implies adequate familiarity with the product. At this stage the client receives information about the existence of the product and its specifications via advertising, trade shows, discussions with other professionals, and salespersons' calls. Samples are shown, documentation is provided, and presentations are made. The industrial client typically carries out an independent search for information about the performance of the product. This stage ends when the client has enough information to decide whether the product should be tested on a pilot basis.

In the next stage, *testing*, limited production runs are performed at the client's plant to evaluate the performance, possible technical problems, and the impact on the cost structure of the client's end product. Following the technical discussions, negotiations start on delivery capabilities and price ranges. Having tested the product thoroughly, the client decides whether the technical and commercial benefits justify purchasing the product for manufacture.

If the decision is positive, the product moves on to the *supplementary source of supply* stage. At this point, it may compete with the present major suppliers and, perhaps, with other supplementary sources of supply. The passage to the next stage, *primary source of supply*, will depend on the performance record of the product and the technical and commercial support of the supplier. Suppliers acting as primary sources are in a

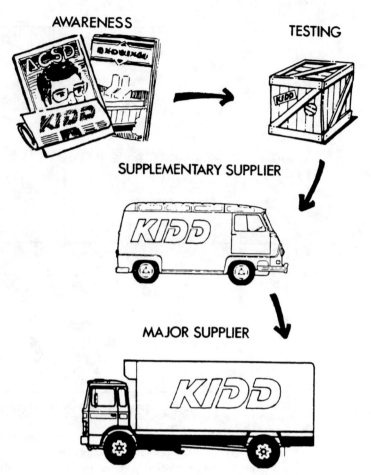

AWARENESS

TESTING

SUPPLEMENTARY SUPPLIER

MAJOR SUPPLIER

Figure 2-5   The purchasing process

privileged position since customers rely heavily on them. Although these stages are consecutive, there may be cases when products leapfrog the supplementary stage if there is a gap for which there are no substitutes on the market.

The DMU structure is typically related to the decision process and the decision makers involved. Each participant may intervene at any stage, given his or her task and concern. For example, one decision maker may be interested in technical matters while another may be involved in commercial considerations.

The differences of concerns and organizational power among decision makers from one stage of adoption to the next may be represented by a matrix form. Exhibit 2-3 displays a fictional example of how this framework may be used in this industry to describe a possible profile of a complete buying process. The stages of the purchasing process are seen horizontally, and each column shows the distribution of involvement of the participants. The example shows how the involvement of the production manager in this particular account is greatly reduced when a product is to be elevated to the primary supplier status. On the other hand, the role of the purchasing manager greatly increases as the firm progresses in the adoption process. The structure of decision making may vary across market segments, implying different approaches in communicating with DMUs at different points in time.

Competition in the Korex market is keen. Supplementary sources sometimes replace primary ones which, in turn, may be disqualified altogether. Therefore a single supplier may simultaneously have different relationships in the market. It may serve as a primary

EXHIBIT 2-3

Framework for Analysis of a Purchasing Process*

Decision maker	Stage of the Adoption Process			
	Awareness (%)	Testing (%)	Supplementary supplier (%)	Primary supplier (%)
Production manager	10	45	45	25
Engineering manager	50	25	10	10
Purchasing manager	30	15	25	35
General manager	10	15	20	30
	100	100	100	100

*This is an example only and these figures are of no use for actual INDUSTRAT decisions.

source to some groups of clients, supplementary to others, or still be in the testing or awareness formation stages or unknown to the rest.

Distribution

Sales by INDUSTRAT firms to customers are done directly, with no middlemen. Purchase orders are given either to salespersons or to their regional offices, which are then responsible for the logistics of delivery and technical support. Although there are some local distributors who carry Korex products, their combined share of the market is insignificant, as they handle either very small customers or intermittent marginal orders.

chapter 3

Administrative Structure of the INDUSTRAT Firm

The organization of a firm represents decisions made on the allocation of tasks and responsibilities in view of the competitive environment. The administrative structure of an INDUSTRAT firm represents the stage of organizational evolution reached in the Korex industry. All five competing firms are organized along similar lines and represent a strong market orientation. In other words, analysis and decisions made by marketing determine the employment of resources in research and development, production, sales, technical support, and other functions.

In order to translate market orientation into profits, each firm's marketing department constitutes a profit center. Decisions made by marketing are aimed at maximizing the firm's profit. This chapter describes the administrative structure governing marketing and its relationships with other departments.

MARKETING AS A PROFIT CENTER

In a competitive market, the posture the firm chooses to take is decisive. Production, finance, and R&D are concerned with the internal workings of the organization. Marketing is the function responsible for the relation of the firm to the external environment. The understanding that the marketing function has of the market and the choices it makes will lead the firm to adopt one posture or another. More specifically, in INDUSTRAT, marketing is responsible for

1. Monitoring market and competitive evolution.
2. Periodically assessing the firm's own strengths and weaknesses.
3. Determining which products should be offered in the long run and what should be the annual R&D effort to develop them, if any.
4. Determining which products, at what prices, should be offered in the short run.
5. Establishing an annual sales forecast.

6. Negotiating with competitors about licensing or other collaborative agreements.
7. Determining the allocation of promotional and support efforts in the field and influencing the orientation of the sales and technical forces.

The annual company report (see Appendix A) reports on the last year's results and the authorized annual expenditure budget by corporate management for the next year. This budget covers R&D projects, promotion, technical support, advertising, sales and technical forces, corporate communication, and marketing research. Although it is not involved in other activities (finance, purchasing, etc.), marketing is responsible for any inefficiencies it may cause due to bad decisions. In such cases, as described next, the losses caused by such inefficiencies are charged against the income contribution that marketing generates.

DETERMINATION OF THE MARKETING BUDGET

Figure 3-1 provides a visual flow of the budgetary structure of marketing. The authorized expenditure budget is spent on payments to other departments within the firm, as well as to outside parties. These expenses are used to generate sales and the resulting net marketing contribution.

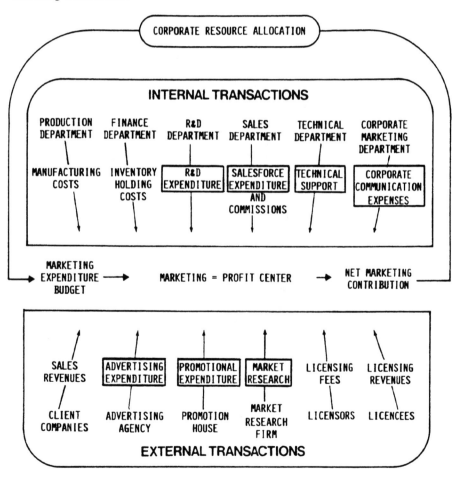

Figure 3-1 The marketing department as a profit center

Corporate management uses the annual net marketing contribution as the source of funds for dividends, debt repayments, investments, and departmental expenditure budgets in the following year. The formula for authorized marketing expenditures takes into account, among other considerations, the contribution marketing generated during the last year. It may be expected that, in case of insufficient contribution, a minimum expenditure budget will be provided for marketing at all times. Beyond this minimum, as contribution rises, the authorized expenditure for the following period will also be increased. However, the growth in authorized marketing expenditures will not grow at the same rate or the growth in contribution. At high levels of contribution, where the absolute level of authorized expenditure is already high, additional authorization would be proportionally lower, while at a low level of contribution they would be higher. As the contribution becomes greater, the proportion allotted to marketing expenditure is thus reduced in order to prevent unnecessary overspending.

The marketing budget may be modified following negotiations between the firm and the INDUSTRAT administrator, who represents either the corporation or other external parties. The administrator evaluates plans presented by the teams and may readjust the budget upward, grant loans, or authorize other arrangements, if convinced of the necessity or desirability of the change. The repayment of loans is deducted from either marketing's contribution to income or from a future expenditure budget at an agreed-upon time.

INTERACTION WITH OTHER DEPARTMENTS

Although the R&D and production departments are profit centers, they may sell their products and services only to marketing. Marketing obtains these products and services via transfer prices and lump sums. Marketing forecasts its next period's sales level for any given product. These forecasts are used by production to plan their level of activity during the year.

Marketing pays the production department for these products only upon sale in the market. Excess inventory is not transferred to the marketing department until it is actually sold to clients. In the meantime an inventory holding cost is charged against the contribution marketing generates. This cost is computed on the basis of a last-in first-out (LIFO) manufacturing cost of the inventory and on the prevailing rate for inventory holding costs. When products are modified or removed from the market, the obsolete inventory write-off is charged to the relevant year's contribution at the current transfer cost.

The working relationship between R&D and marketing is such that marketing specifies projects for R&D to perform. Each project is defined by technical specifications and an annual allocation of funds from the marketing expenditure budget. Other major production and R&D investments are funded directly by corporate management, and marketing has no control over how these funds are spent. However, corporate outlays normally try to sustain the strategies pursued by marketing.

chapter 4

Information for Industrial Marketing Strategies

INDUSTRAT was designed to enable the formulation and execution of strategy over several years in a competitive environment. The competing firms must deal with the long and short term, and make the necessary trade-offs when the two are in conflict. Since the simulation is strategically oriented, some short term tactical issues, such as the negotiation process with individual customers, have been delegated to lower echelons in the organization.

There are two levels of management decisions in INDUSTRAT:

1. Resource allocation by major strategic programs (products, market segments, and technologies) and
2. Marketing mix decisions.

The first level represents the firm's commitments, that is, investments and risks for at least one complete year. The second level represents a shorter run execution question. At both levels, choices made by the marketing department involve activities in the other departments implementing these choices.

The nature of the INDUSTRAT marketplace is dynamic; customers' needs may change as may their pre rences. INDUSTRAT firms constantly evaluate the market and plan strategic and tactical steps. At the same time, the pattern of interaction between customers' behavior and competitive actions is also influenced by the economic and regulatory environments.

Strategy formulation and execution require continuous information-gathering about the INDUSTRAT environment and its structure. Some of the information is covered in this manual. However, observing customers' and competitors' behavior is a crucial task performed independently by each firm's management team. To this end, formal information is available about the market via a free industry newsletter and through commercial market research studies designed to monitor the evolution of the market. A list of the studies available is displayed in Exhibit 4-1.

EXHIBIT 4-1

Market Research Studies Available

---

1. Supplier Survey
2. Survey on Perception of Suppliers
3. Product Awareness & Preference Survey: Korex Market
4. Demand Analysis: Korex Market
5. Market Shares Survey: Korex Market
6. Survey of Organizational Buying Processes: Korex Market
7. Semantic Scales on Product Perception: Korex Market
8. Perceptual Map of Products: Korex Market
9. Market Forecast: Korex Market
10. Product Awareness & Preference Survey: Lomex Market
11. Demand Analysis: Lomex Market
12. Market Shares Survey: Lomex Market
13. Survey of Organizational Buying Processes: Lomex Market
14. Semantic Scales on Product Perception: Lomex Market
15. Market Forecast: Lomex Market
16. Competitive Information

The purchase price of each market research study is announced before the beginning of each year. This cost is automatically charged to the firm's marketing expenditure budget and is included in the annual company report. The remainder of this chapter will discuss how market research information in INDUSTRAT may be used for the analysis of segmentation, positioning, and the market's dynamics. These specimen studies are presented in Appendix B.

MARKET SEGMENTATION AND CUSTOMER NEEDS

The essence of market segmentation is that members of a segment have similar needs which are, on the average, significantly different from those of other segments. By aiming the marketing program on a market segment, the firm expects the segment to perceive that its offering fits its needs more than other competitive offerings. On the other hand, by trying to attract several segments simultaneously with only one marketing program this differentiation is compromised.

The dimension used to classify buyers into segments is a *segmentation scheme*. The scheme may follow two different directions. It may

1. identify groups that manifest different purchasing behaviors, find the characteristics of the group that relate to these preferences, and define a segmentation scheme accordingly, or
2. identify groups with different characteristics and search for purchasing behavior differences relating to these characteristics.

Companies generally follow a mixture of both approaches over time, resulting in a segmentation scheme with which management feels comfortable. If the segmentation scheme parallels the different purchasing behaviors of the segments, the scheme will be strategically meaningful. Decisions may then be taken as to how to adapt to each of the segments. On the other hand, a segmentation scheme reflecting similar behavior across the segments may cause duplication of effort. A common approach to such segments would be more economical.

The evolution of customer needs and competitive activity may call for the use of different segmentation schemes. For example, while customers may be sensitive to product quality today, they may be more sensitive to service tomorrow. Need priority may evolve differently in different segments; the needs may either converge or grow apart over time. Such changes may render a segmentation scheme obsolete and require the adoption of another for future strategy. INDUSTRAT firms may use three macrosegmentation schemes: *geography, size of the account,* and the *end product.*

As seen in Appendix B, market research information in INDUSTRAT may be presented according to only one of the macrosegmentation schemes (see Figure 4-1). It is management's choice as to which would be most useful. The firm may ask the suppliers of market research to investigate which macrosegmentation scheme would reveal significant differences between the behaviors of the segments.

The market researchers then analyze the similarity among the measurements within and between the segments for each segmentation scheme. The scheme regarded as optimal is the one in which there is a maximum of similarity within the segments, and a maximum of dissimilarity between the segments' averages. The scheme yielding the most such intergroup differences is presented by the market research supplier as optimal. This is merely a statistical optimum, and the firm may prefer to disregard it and to use other segmentation schemes.

When ordering a market research study, the firm must specify one macrosegmentation scheme by which it would like to have the data displayed. The codes of the alternative macrosegmentation schemes are

1—Aggregate statistics only

2—Geographical segments

3—Customer size segments

4—End product segments

5—Statistically optimal segmentation schemes

The firm's choice here will have an impact on the market research costs. This cost is based on the methodology used and the sample size necessary for meaningful results. Segmentation implies a separate independent study for each segment, thus increasing the necessary sample size. An optimal segmentation study requires a special analysis, which makes the study more expensive. More specifically, the basic cost of a study, based on aggregate statistics, is multiplied by a factor of 1.5 for a macrosegmentation scheme and by a factor of 2.0 for an optimal macrosegmentation scheme.

END PRODUCT

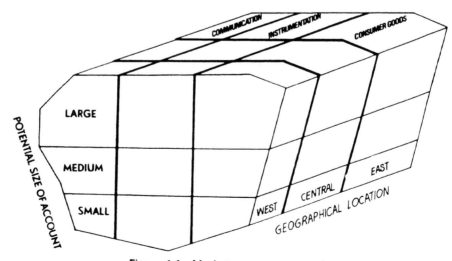

Figure 4-1   Market macrosegmentation

POSITIONING OF COMPETING SUPPLIERS

Physical specifications of products are the basis for satisfying needs in the marketplace. Yet a firm's success may result only partly from its products' quality. The purchasing of industrial products is, in many cases, part of a relationship that goes beyond the product, although in the longer run a fit at the product level is a prerequisite for a good relationship.

The choice of product commits the customer for at least the short run. Switching costs are high in many cases, since a typical customer will adapt the production system to a particular set of specifications. Similarly, his or her customers may have to adapt their production process to the changes. A purchasing decision is thus a commitment to a relationship and the decision to enter into it or to discontinue it is made cautiously by customers. Market Research Study 1. *Supplier Survey*, provides information about awareness of clients and preferences for the five suppliers present on the market.[2] The individuals questioned are samples of decision makers in client organizations.

Each customer is concerned with, in addition to the quality of the product and its price, the continuity of supply, the technical support, the reputation of the supplier, strategic information provided, the quality of the suppliers' sales force, and other ancillary services. Market research experience in this industry has grouped these various concerns into three general dimensions and labelled them

1. Technical aspects (TEC)
2. Commercial aspects (COM)
3. General reputation of the corporation (REP)

The relative importance of these dimensions may vary by decision makers, applications, and current competitive conditions. A customer would first try to satisfy high priority needs before considering low priority ones. Study 2, *Survey on Perceptions of Suppliers*, provides information on the positioning of competing suppliers in INDUSTRAT as perceived by decision makers in the market. The relative importance of the three dimensions (TEC, COM, and REP) is given by percentage. Each respondent in this study is asked to represent his or her requirements by rating, on a scale of 1 to 7 for each dimension, his or her *ideal supplier*.[3] The respondent then rates each one of the competing suppliers by the same scale.

When combined with the ideal points, the supplier ratings yield the positioning of the competing suppliers in a perceptual space reflecting customer needs, requirements, and preferences. Other things being equal, the respondent would prefer to do business with the supplier closest to the ideal point. The figures provided in the study are averages of the responses for the decision makers in each macrosegment.

PRODUCT FAMILIARITY AND PREFERENCES

Study 3, *Product Awareness and Preference Survey: Korex Market*, provides information about decision makers' familiarity with and relative interest in the products offered on the market. The first table shows the percentage of the respondents who showed awareness of the products in each market segment. The next table displays the preferences that respondents have shown for the products offered on the market.

[2]*Awareness*, in this study measures spontaneous, unaided recall. Thus, respondents may not mention all the suppliers, although they are familiar with them. *Preference* is based on considering all competitors. Interviewers remind their respondents of the availability of the competing suppliers before the question on choice is posed.

[3]The term *ideal* represents, in the jargon of market researchers, the profile of the most suitable supplier. Questioning techniques assure that the respondent, when thinking of such a supplier, takes realistic tradeoffs into account. In other words, the posture of an ideal supplier represents the maximum satisfaction which the client expects while not trading away the supplier's economic survival.

MARKET STRUCTURE

Because customers are cautious about their choices of supply, an important objective to a supplier may be to achieve the status of a major source of supply, which represents a relatively strong client relationship. Study 4, *Demand Analysis: Korex Market*, monitors the status of primary sourcing behavior by clients. It first displays the size of the market by the number of prospective clients, their global purchasing for the period in value and unit volume, and the average value per client. This information is displayed for the overall market and for market segments. The study then gives the percentages of purchases originating from suppliers designated as *primary suppliers*, with the balance of purchases bought from supplementary suppliers. Finally, the last figure represents the average number of suppliers per customer in the market.

MARKET SHARES

Market research allows the monitoring of the performance of different products along the three chronological stages of the adoption process, testing, supplementary, and primary sources. Each product is in one of the three stages with each client. It may be useful to see how the product is performing if customers at each of the stages are examined separately. Study 5, *Market Shares Survey: Korex Market*, estimates the proportion of accounts that were testing each product and the accounts that used them as supplementary and as primary sources of supply. For example, the same product may have a low share of clients who are testing a variety of products, a high share of clients in the supplementary stage, and a low share of clients at the primary stage.

ORGANIZATIONAL BUYING PROCESSES

Client organizations of INDUSTRAT firms usually involve four major decision makers who participate in the purchasing process. The formulation and execution of strategy may be improved when the relative influences of these participants are taken into account. Study 6, *Survey of Organizational Buying Processes: Korex Market*, estimates the relative weights of the different decision makers in the buying decision. These weights may differ across market segments.

The information in this study pertains to all stages of the product adoption process. However, industry experience indicates that there are differences in the relative influence of certain decision makers across the stages of the process. The reason lies in the different tasks and responsibilities which engineers, production, purchasing, and general managers have at those stages. The problems with which a client organization is concerned at the testing and investigation stage are naturally different from those at later stages. For example, a large part of the initial concerns may be product specific while later problems may revolve around the wider scope of a client–supplier relationship.

Unfortunately, market research methodology in this industry has not yet been able to provide a reliable distinction between the relative roles of decision makers at the different stages of adoption. Nevertheless, the fact that market research has not yet captured these differences should not reduce the plausibility of this phenomenon.

PERCEPTUAL PRODUCT POSITIONING

Each product in INDUSTRAT may be specified according to numerous physical performance characteristics. According to industry experience, customers consider five characteristics of each product category to be the most significant; four are physical and the fifth financial. For Korex products, the physical ones are resistance, suspension, frequency, and density. For Lomex, they are convexity, conductivity, purity, and maximum energy. The fifth characteristic for both products is the cost associated with their applications. Research experience indicates that three of the five factors are rated by clients as being of crucial priority for both Korex and Lomex. Respondents usually require satisfaction from these three dimensions first, before comparing competing products on either of the other two characteristics.

The first part of Study 7, *Semantic Scales on Product Perception: Korex Market* displays the identity and relative importance of each of these three attributes. While the other two physical characteristics remain significant, the importance of the three displayed in this study seems to justify the elimination of all others from current studies, according to market researchers. Industry experts expect, however, that the other physical characteristics may become more important to customers in the future. When that happens, market research will detect this phenomenon, and display another set of three physical characteristics.

The study provides product perception information on the three attributes. It displays the ideal points, which represent the performance needs of customers considering their applications, and the ratings each competing product received from respondents. The closer a product's rating is perceived to be to the ideal point of a market segment, the more it should satisfy the product needs of the decision makers who were interviewed in this study. This alone does not assure better sales performance, because other factors influence the purchasing process.

Study 8, *Perceptual Map of Products: Korex Market*, is a study using an alternative method for measuring perceptual positioning of products. In the previous study the respondent rated separately each of the products along specific individual physical characteristics. Another way to question the respondent is to avoid specific dimensions and ask about the overall similarity and dissimilarity of the products. This method, called *Multidimensional Scaling*,[4] leaves the choice of the specific dimensions of the product and their relative importance to the respondent's discretion. It yields an overall similarity measure between products, resulting in a graphical presentation of a perceptual map. This map displays the products offered on the market, and the ideal points of market segments. As in Study 7, the shorter the distance to the ideal point the higher the respondent's satisfaction should be with the product.

The study presents two-dimensional maps that satisfy certain statistical testing procedures. Since the data is based on the measurement of overall similarity perceptions, rather than on separate comparisons of specific characteristics, the meaning of each axis on the map is usually interpreted by the market researcher's familiarity with the market, expert judgement, and statistical analysis. In INDUSTRAT, the interpretation of the two coordinates yielded by this methodology resulted from analysis of the similarity between positions on the two axes in this map and the dimensions that emerged as most important in Study 7.

The numbers on the map represent ideal points for the four decision makers usually involved. The letters represent the perceived positioning of the twenty best selling products in descending order of sales volume. *A* represents the largest selling product, *B* the next best seller, and so on. The map does not include less popular products for which there are too few responses.

Positioning information allows the evaluation of various strategic alternatives. Products may be repositioned, withdrawn, introduced, or retained at the same position in view of past, present, and anticipated competitive developments. Repositioning a product may be done by changing product characteristics considered important by customers, such as

[4]For a presentation of non-metric multidimensional techniques see Thomas C. Kinnear and James R. Taylor, *Marketing Research: An Applied Approach*, 2nd edition. New York, NY: McGraw-Hill Book Company, 1983.

price and other physical characteristics. This may require completion of R&D projects to make the changed physical product and its production process available.

The semantic scales and map are only perceptual measurements, and careful analysis should relate perceptual positioning to the actual physical characteristics of the products. Sometimes customers' perceptions may distort the positioning that a supplier designs a product to have in the marketplace. This implies that perceptual positioning is the result of the combined efforts of R&D and other, communication oriented, functions.

Repositioning a product through changes in its physical characteristics is only one alternative for taking advantage of a market opportunity. The marketing department may decide to launch a new product altogether, while retaining or eliminating a present offering. A modified product will reap the benefits of the users' familiarity with it. On the other hand, a drastic repositioning of a product may be difficult after a long history of entrenchment in a certain perceived market position.

Perceptual positioning of products is one of many factors contributing to market performance. For example, two competing products may not be selling in amounts proportional to their respective distances from the ideal points. This may be due to problems of market awareness of the product offered, or to difficulties in other elements of the relationship of suppliers with current and prospective customers.

TURE KOREX MARKET SIZE AND COMPETITION

Study 9, *Market Forecast: Korex Market*, provides a forecast of the future size of the market and its segments, based on econometric statistical methods. As with many other methodologies, these techniques may be at fault. Over time each INDUSTRAT team will become more familiar with the market, enabling it to better evaluate econometrically-based forecasts in view of anticipated developments.

UDIES ON THE LOMEX MARKET

The Lomex market is a separate and independent market from Korex, based on a different technology, different clients, and different needs. There is no interaction between the two markets at the buying level. In other words, Lomex purchase decisions would not affect Korex nor vice versa. However, both products, if offered by a competing IN-DUSTRAT firm, use common resources. Therefore, action on the Korex market may have an impact on the Lomex market and vice versa through the firms' strategic choices and the scarcity of their resources.

Because the Lomex market is currently nonexistent, there is obviously no experience in its market analysis. Nonetheless, the industry expects to retain the three macrosegmentation schemes used in the Korex market, as they are generally applicable to such industrial marketing situations. However, since there are no Lomex products on the market, there are no records of applications in end products, rate of adoption, or market potential. Although end use is expected to be a viable segmentation scheme, the actual uses are still unknown.

The market research studies pertaining to the Lomex market follow the format and methodology of those studies on the Korex market. They are

Study 10. *Product Awareness and Preference Survey: Lomex Market*
Study 11. *Demand Analysis: Lomex Market*
Study 12. *Market Shares Survey: Lomex Market*
Study 13. *Survey of Organizational Buying Processes: Lomex Market*

Study 14. *Semantic Scales on Product Perception: Lomex Market*

Study 15. *Market Forecast: Lomex Market*

No perceptual maps are available for this market, as it is expected that the number of Lomex products on the market will not be sufficient in the course of the simulation to conduct a multidimensional scaling study. As long as there are no Lomex products on the market, studies 10, 11, and 12 are irrelevant. Study 12 is also irrelevant when there is only one Lomex product on the market. So, it would be a waste of funds to order these studies when they are of no analytical value.

COMPETITIVE ACTIVITY

Monitoring and anticipating competitive action is indispensable for strategy formulation and execution. Some information on competing activities is public knowledge. For example, the launch of a new product, the change of physical specifications of a current product, and price changes are all visible actions. Special marketing activities of a competitor in support of a product line are more difficult to observe. In this industry, as in many others, specialized sources are available which monitor competitive behavior. Study 16, *Competitive Information*, provides information compiled from trade journals, publicly available industry studies, and other sources.

The study begins by displaying information on competitors' decisions with respect to each of their products. For each product on the market the table displays the corre-

OBJECTIVES :

UNDERSTANDING MARKETS
MONITORING
IDENTIFYING THREATS & OPPORTUNITIES
FORECASTING

METHODOLOGY :

ANALYSIS OF SURVEY DATA

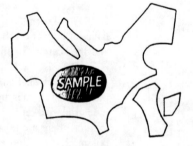

MARKET SEGMENTATION :

NONE, SPECIFIED OR STATISTICAL

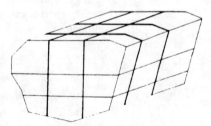

Figure 4-2 Market research

sponding decisions on maximum price discounts, promotional budgets, sales force commission, technical support, and advertising. This information is a result of research and estimation and it may necessarily include some error. A way for the analyst to ascertain this is to compare his or her own product management decisions with the corresponding estimates.

The rest of the study provides competitors' corporate information where the application to specific products is difficult to determine. For every firm, the study shows an estimate of the size of the sales and technical forces, their respective training budgets, and the estimated corporate marketing outlay. The study concludes with the estimated allocations of competitors' sales and technical support efforts over the three macrosegmentation and one microsegmentation schemes.

It must be emphasized that problems of reliability and validity, which are usually present in survey research, may also be present in the studies sold to INDUSTRAT firms in the course of the simulation. Market research in the INDUSTRAT world is also based on samples of individuals responding to questionnaires and interviewers. However, in order to improve the firm's capability to understand the market, monitor and forecast developments, and identify threats and opportunities, the benefits of market research studies must be accepted together with their weaknesses. As the firm gains familiarity with the market it will develop an appreciation for the value of certain studies and their reliability. Naturally, as market research suppliers gain experience in providing information about a market, the information stands to be more reliable (see Figure 4-2). For example, one should expect that market research on Korex should be more reliable at this stage than for Lomex, since not much information is available yet.

chapter 5

Execution of Industrial Marketing Strategies

Following strategic choices, programs must be designed to market the products that the firm plans to offer on the market. For every product offered, the production department must be given a sales forecast to which it will be prepared to respond. All products require a marketing program covering all the elements of the marketing mix. Other programs of action must be specified for the sales and technical forces, corporate marketing, and R&D. The choices made at the strategic level may also involve negotiation for licensing or other collaborative arrangements with competitors.

PRODUCT DECISIONS

Manufacturing methods in this industry have evolved over the years in an effort to adapt to sales fluctuations. Two important characteristics of the current approach allow considerable flexibility. The first is in the use of subcontracting. By having unrestricted access to subcontractors on an annual basis, the competing firms in INDUSTRAT are not bound to longer term commitments for capacity levels.

The second characteristic is the flexibility in current manufacturing systems, allowing a relatively easy change between Korex and Lomex products and their various technologies. However, production may manufacture only products for which R&D has been successful in providing the technology and manufacturing specifications. With this prerequisite satisfied, production will be able to provide the annual volume requested by marketing, and to operate at this requested level for one year.

Although production is flexible from year to year, the annual volume requested for a product represents a commitment for the year. On the other hand this request is based on a sales forecast which may be erroneous. In view of this possibility a marginal flexibility has been developed. If sales are within a 20 percent deviation from marketing's forecast, production will automatically adjust the requested annual production level to that point during the year with no additional costs.

Under such conditions no excess inventory will remain at the year's end. If sales are more than 20 percent below the requested production, excess inventory will be shown. Its size will be the difference between 80 percent of the original request and the actual sales for this product. If demand is more than 20 percent over the forecast, a maximum upward production adjustment of 20 percent will take place. Any sales that the firm could have made for this product beyond this augmented volume will thus be lost.

According to the INDUSTRAT firm's administrative process, it is only when products are actually sold to the customers that marketing pays production for them at transfer cost. Under these conditions, marketing is not charged for the manufacturing cost of excess inventory, should there be any. However, the holding costs of this inventory such as interest, space, and insurance, will be charged against marketing's annual contribution because it will be held responsible for the forecasting error and the resulting inefficiency. The actual cost of the inventory is carried, until sold, on the books of the production department at current cost (LIFO) value. If marketing decides to discontinue a brand or to modify it by using a new set of R&D specifications, the costs of any existing obsolete inventory will automatically be charged to marketing as an annual exceptional cost.

The costs of manufacturing a product depend on how it is manufactured and the experience with that production process. Production methods are determined by the development department through development projects that are requested and financed by the marketing department. These projects provide the development department with a set of specific physical characteristics for the product and a desired corresponding cost base. The cost base will be reached if the results of this development project are implemented by the production department and production has an experience of approximately 100,000 in cumulative production.

The manufacturing costs per unit are expected to be higher than base cost if cumulative production has not reached the 100,000 mark. However, as the production department follows development's specifications, cost per unit will be lower than base cost once cumulative production is beyond 100,000 units. If the expected cost reduction resulting from cumulative experience is not viewed as strategically sufficient, marketing may call on the development department to launch a cost reduction project for lowering the base cost, for the same set of physical specifications, to the desired level. The new manufacturing method will be operational only when the project is adopted by production.

As the production department transfers its manufacturing experience from one product to another, the calculation of cumulative production takes into account all manufacturing within the same technology. Thus when a new development project is employed, it already enjoys all the production experience accumulated in the firm across the use of the same technology (1, 2, 3, or 4 for Korex and 5 for Lomex). This would give each product within the given technology a similar cumulative production for calculating the relevant experience. However, the base cost for the experience curve is determined uniquely by the development project that was employed. On the other hand, if a development project uses a technology new to the firm, the cumulative production figure will include only the manufacturing that used the new technology (see Figure 5-1).

In some cases, for various given specifications, the firm may already be producing a product at its minimum base cost, that is, by the most efficient production method. In such instances further cost reduction would only occur due to cumulative production experience. Production reports regularly to R&D on the product's costs. This information helps in the design of production methods for future products with similar specifications.

The reduction of base cost via a development project is regarded in this industry as a product modification. Although the four physical specifications, which are considered most important from the market's point of view, remain unchanged, others must be altered by the development department. Customers do detect such minor alterations and insist on having the most recent version of the product. This makes any inventory, which was manufactured prior to implementation of the successful cost reduction project, obsolete and unsaleable in this market. The administrative system of the firm will automatically

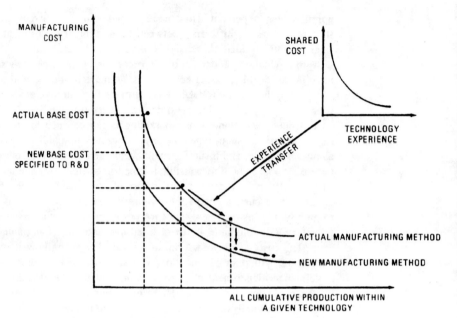

Figure 5-1   Production costs

charge the manufacturing costs of this inventory to marketing's operational contribution, and transfer the funds to production, the department that had invested in building this inventory on behalf of marketing.

In order to not discourage cost reduction projects or any other modification of existing products, INDUSTRAT simulation administrators may authorize an exceptional transaction with a firm's production department. For example, the administrator may pay production for part or all of the obsolete inventory and export it out of the INDUSTRAT market.

PRODUCT MARKETING PROGRAMS

Along with the production request, the marketing department must make decisions concerning the marketing mix for each product. The elements of the marketing mix in the INDUSTRAT simulation are list price, maximum price discount, promotion, sales commission, product advertising, and allocation of technical support.

List Price

This is the official price per unit quoted to all customers. Once a list price is determined, drastic annual changes are not acceptable since they damage the supplier's credibility. However, a yearly variation of up to approximately 30 percent has proven to be a feasible price change in this market.

Maximum Price Discount

The product list price represents marketing's overall competitive considerations. However, salespersons in the field may find that competition in certain territories is more intense than expected. To support them in such situations, marketing may authorize an autonomous decision by the salesperson on a percentage discount off list price. The more skillful and trained a salesperson is, the smaller the discounts he or she is expected to yield. Nevertheless, in order to retain its competitive position, marketing will not authorize discounts beyond 10 percent. So far, the average discount has amounted to around 5 percent of the list price.

Sales Force Commission

Salespersons in this industry are paid partly by salary and partly by sales commission. The commission is a constant percentage of the net sales revenues generated and is regarded as an incentive. When management feels that the role of the sales force is relatively important, it may increase this product's sales commission. But, in cases where the sales force's role is minor, management may wish to spend the earned contribution margin in another way. Industry experience of sales force commission shows an average of 5 percent with a maximum of 20 percent.

Promotion

While the sales force deals directly with individual customers, marketing may undertake promotional activities to support the sales effort. These include participation in trade shows, distribution of free product samples, and particular sales campaigns. The decision on what promotional tools will actually be employed is delegated to lower management. However, the marketing department must decide what the total promotional budget for the year will be for each product.

Product Advertising

Marketing may allocate an advertising budget to each individual product. INDUSTRAT firms work with specialized advertising agencies who operate within a budget in the most effective way. There are no advertising restrictions, but the industry has traditionally avoided consumer oriented mass media. Advertising has concentrated on brochures, trade publications, business supplements, and other industrial vehicles. While advertising budgets are relatively low, it is recognized that advertising does play an important role at certain stages in a product's life cycle. The actual execution of advertising in terms of message content and media mix is delegated to lower management, who, in their analysis, automatically employ the ideal points of the target segments chosen by the firm.

SALES FORCE DECISIONS

The role of the salesperson is to prospect for new accounts, follow the purchasing process within them, negotiate prices, and coordinate the technical and commercial relationship with the client after the sale is made. Each salesperson in INDUSTRAT sells the full range of products offered by his or her firm. It is not possible for marketing to dictate the allocation of the individual salesperson's time or efforts. In fact, the sales force is a separate organization, independent of marketing, within the firm. Beyond varied sales commissions, the marketing department can influence the sales force only by determining its organizational structure and by providing training budgets and guidelines on salespersons' time allocation.

For instance, the marketing department may wish the sales force to spend certain proportions of contact time across each of the segmentation schemes. Marketing may want the sales force to focus on the East and to devote less attention, though not neglect, the other two regions. Simultaneously, the department may want to concentrate on the larger accounts, but maintain a significant proportion of contacts with the smaller accounts. At the same time, marketing sees all three end product segments as equally important. Finally, marketing may want the sales force to divide its time between the purchasing and general managers and virtually ignore the other decision makers during the year.

Marketing directs the sales department on how to allocate its resources across each of the segmentation schemes. It must, however, choose a single macrosegmentation scheme by which the sales force will be organized. This guarantees an allocation of resources across this one scheme in accordance with marketing's wishes. The codes representing the schemes by which the sales force may be organized are 1 for geography, 2 for account size, and 3 for end product.

Once a macrosegmentation scheme is adopted as an organizational structure, the sales force will strictly follow the proportions along this scheme. For example, consider a firm that decides to employ 50 salespersons and adopts a geographical organization. If marketing desired 30 percent of the sales force resources to be dedicated to the eastern region, 15 salespersons would be assigned to this segment. Within this organization, each salesperson will try to follow the proportion specified by marketing for the other macrosegmentation and microsegmentation schemes. For instance, in a geographically organized sales force, marketing may request 50 percent of sales force resources on large accounts. The individual salesperson, already assigned to a geographical segment, would try to implement this request.

It is impossible to control the way a salesperson manages his or her time and relationships with individual accounts. An organizational form assures a certain desired allocation scheme and the rest is managed by guidelines only. However, a more highly trained sales force would be capable of understanding the strategic marketing issues and the ensuing guidelines. It is likely then that higher sales force training budgets will improve the sales force's adherence to the proportions of time allocation, which marketing cannot assure via an organizational scheme.

The sales force expenditure budget must cover the total number of salespersons as well as their hiring, firing, and training costs. A first-year salesperson will incur both hiring costs, which include routine sales and technical training, and salary. A departing salesperson will only incur firing costs. Such costs are similar for all five firms and will be announced each year in the industry's newsletter. The training budget is a marketing decision, as changing competitive situations may require new product or segment-oriented training programs.

The relationships of salespersons with their clients takes time to evolve and every reorganization entails relocation and the need to establish new relationships. Reorganization and reassignment of the sales force may cause a temporary loss of sales force effectiveness. It is up to the management of each firm to consider the prospective benefits in the light of the temporary loss of rapport with customers in the marketplace.

TECHNICAL SUPPORT

In the process of adopting new products or changing production methods, customers may encounter technical problems that their personnel cannot resolve. The role of technical support is to render assistance in such cases mainly through visits by qualified technicians. The size of the technical force, its training budget, and allocation across products and market segments are marketing's decisions. Technicians are trained to support all the products that the company offers.

The allocation guidelines are firstly product oriented, indicating what percentage of the technical support budget should go to each of the products. Simultaneously, marketing may have other strategic inputs into this allocation decision, relating to the segmentation of the market. For example, while devoting 50 percent of the technical support resources to a certain product, marketing may also want to emphasize the importance of large accounts across the whole line.

The allocation of the technical force to market segments does not necessarily have to resemble that of the sales force. However, in the interest of coordination, the organizational structure of technical support will automatically follow the one chosen for the sales force. This implies that after the product criterion, the macrosegmentation chosen as an organizational scheme will be of highest priority for the allocation of technical support resources.

The expenses involved in hiring and firing technicians are similar for all five firms and will be announced in the industry newsletter. The training budget should be related to the technical support expected in the field during the year, and should improve the implementation of marketing's guidelines.

ORPORATE MARKETING

Corporate marketing bolsters the credibility of the firm as a supplier in the marketplace. It is difficult to relate this activity to specific products or segments. In the past, annual corporate communications budgets, consisting mostly of public relations campaigns, have been significantly lower than the total advertising budgets spent specifically on individual products. The actual execution of a corporate communication program is delegated to lower management, who automatically consider the ideal points of the segments used by the firm.

ESEARCH AND DEVELOPMENT

The marketing department of an INDUSTRAT firm may request the R&D department to take on specific projects in order to improve existing products or to introduce new ones. Various combinations of characteristics are made possible by different technologies. If the desired combination of physical characteristics is within a range of a technology to which the firm has access, a development project may be launched. Marketing specifies a project name, an annual budget, physical characteristics sought, and the target base cost for that configuration. It must be sure that the firm possesses the basic technology to develop the new product. If the firm does not possess this prerequisite, it will have to first invest in research for the technology to become available.

Research

Both Korex and Lomex product categories are the result of basic scientific research. The development of commercially viable products represents a process which goes well beyond science into specific industrial applications. This process culminates in a successful *development project*, where the R&D department transfers to production the necessary know-how to manufacture the product. Simultaneously, R&D prepares the technical support department for certain difficulties that clients may have in adopting the product.

However, both Korex and Lomex must first pass the technology research stage. The reason for this intermediate stage is that, although science has prepared a theoretical base for developing products, the industrial and commercial implementation of certain specifications is difficult. Combining some physical properties requires a certain technology before the consideration of production methods.

Korex products may be based on four different technologies. Each of these is applicable to a combination of certain ranges of product specifications. Each technology only serves as a basis for product development within a defined specification range. However, since technologies may overlap, more than one may constitute the base for the development of a product with similar performance characteristics.

Exhibit 5-1 displays the possible product specifications which are covered by each of the four Korex technologies. As far as the Lomex product category is concerned, there

EXHIBIT 5-1

Korex Technologies

Technology lower and upper limits	Resistance (Ω)	Suspension (μs)	Frequency (kHz)	Density ($\mu g/mm^3$)
1. Minimum	500	15	30	500
Maximum	4500	55	200	800
2. Minimum	2000	10	30	500
Maximum	12000	60	200	800
3. Minimum	1000	45	30	500
Maximum	4000	105	200	800
4. Minimum	2500	40	30	500
Maximum	10000	100	200	800

is not yet enough experience in R&D to differentiate between specification ranges. However, since Lomex is only a scientific development at this time, industrial technology must be made available before a commercial product is developed. At this time, it is believed that this technology will cover the whole range for Lomex physical specifications.

Research for technology is a time- and resource-consuming process. A team of researchers, who will contribute their experience to the effort must be gathered and built. This group of highly paid scientists and engineers must be provided with the proper infrastructure, good quality research facilities, and staff. The need for a critical mass is expressed by the minimum requirements for funds and elapsed time before a technology is available to a firm. Industry experts can usually estimate the minimum annual investments necessary for successful technology research. Similarly, these experts are in a position to determine the number of years that the search for a given technology should last before it is likely to be successful.

Exhibit 5-2 shows these minimum requirements for each of the Lomex and four Korex technologies. Each year the research department communicates to marketing the minimum annual, minimum total, and the proposed investments necessary for the successful development of each technology. Spending below the minimum annual investment would not be a total waste of funds. Although it would have no effect on the number of years necessary for research, it would reduce the future total investment required to gain access to the technology.

Research aimed at developing new technologies represents a heavy commitment of financial resources and scientific expertise. As in many science based industries, a critical mass is essential for the accumulation of research experience. In order to enable researchers

EXHIBIT 5-2

Requirements for Technological Research

Technology	Minimum years of research	Minimum annual budget* ($)	Minimum total budget* ($)	Minimum budget* for a development project ($)
1	1	1000	3200	150
2	2	1600	5400	250
3	2	1600	5400	250
4	2	2200	8700	550
5	2	2200	11000	550

*The financial amounts are expressed at the current values of the opening period.

to have this necessary focus, INDUSTRAT firms only engage in the pursuit of a single technology in any given year.

Development

Successful technological research would enable the firm to proceed with the development of products within new ranges of specifications. This activity would be in the form of development projects following product specifications set by the marketing department, which would determine the specifications according to strategic considerations.

Marketing must decide what to allocate from its expenditure budget for investment in development projects. In addition to the target specifications of the project sought, marketing must specify the technology on which to base the project. R&D will proceed to evaluate the project's technical feasibility, determine the necessary budgets and develop a prototype run of the product specifying the raw materials and production methods.

A development project is designated by an internal project code or name, consisting of five letters. The first letter is P, for project; the second letter represents the category of product to be developed, K for Korex and L for Lomex. The third letter identifies the firm carrying out the project, A, E, I, O, and U for firms one through five. The last two letters in the project name are selected by the firm as an internal code for project identification. For example, PKAXX and PLAZZ are names of Korex and Lomex development projects, respectively, belonging to firm one.

The twenty products currently on the market are the result of twenty development projects. The project names are the present product names preceded by the letter P. For example, firm three's product KISS was launched according to the specifications of project PKISS. All INDUSTRAT firms used a similar name convention in the past.

This implies that each team in the simulation has four successfully completed development projects at its disposal. These represent specifications of physical characteristics and a corresponding production method for a base cost. Each project may be used for the modification of a product which is currently on the market or for a new product introduction.

The lower the target base cost, the more difficult it will be for R&D to develop a product. Once a development project is complete, this cost corresponds to the transfer cost between production and marketing at the 100,000th unit produced. Above this mark the transfer cost will decrease with production experience, and below it, it will be considerably higher.

A maximum of four development projects is allowed each year. Once they are launched, R&D will annually report to marketing on the status of each project and the funds necessary to complete them, if unfinished (see Figure 5-2). If there has been overbudgeting on a project, R&D will use the balance within its internal activities and will not report the difference. An unfinished development project may be completed at a later date and at a spending rate chosen by the marketing department.

A project in progress must always keep its original name and physical characteristics, as a changed name implies a new project. A change in any physical characteristic will be ignored as long as the project carries the same name. The base cost may be adjusted at any time in order to release cost constraints and increase the likelihood of a project's success. The development group would update the base cost automatically in case of inflation (see Figure 5-3).

Marketing may discontinue development projects and resume them whenever necessary while retaining the results of work done up to that point. Experience gained from one development project is transferred to future development projects. Such a transfer will increase the firm's capabilities to complete projects with similar physical characteristics on lower budgets and lower base costs. However, this experience transfer will only take place after the successful completion of the preceding project.

PERIOD T : PROJECT SPECIFICATION : { PROJECT NAME

TECHNOLOGY

BUDGET

4 PHYSICAL CHARACTERISTICS

PRODUCTION BASE COST

↓ ↓

MESSAGE FROM R&D : { PROJECT STATUS

FEASIBILITY OF BASE COST

ADDITIONAL BUDGET NECESSARY

PERIOD T + 1 : ACTION

Figure 5-2 Product development

PROJECT NAME

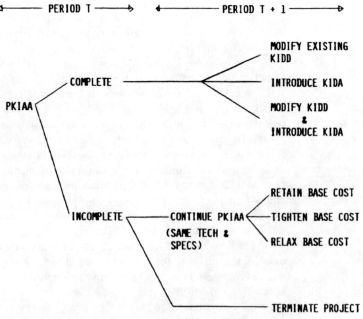

◄───── PERIOD T ─────►   ◄───── PERIOD T + 1 ─────►

MODIFY EXISTING
KIDD

COMPLETE ─────────────── INTRODUCE KIDA

PKIAA

MODIFY KIDD
&
INTRODUCE KIDA

RETAIN BASE COST

INCOMPLETE ─── CONTINUE PKIAA ◄─TIGHTEN BASE COST
            (SAME TECH &
            SPECS)   RELAX BASE COST

TERMINATE PROJECT

Figure 5-3 Development—Project name

Since the successful completion of a development project is influenced by the cumulative expenditure, marketing may time the investments in a project according to its available resources and strategic needs. Both the base cost and the amount requested by R&D to complete projects are given in current monetary values.

Development projects may be used to reduce the base cost for on-going products. This may happen when production experience effects on costs are insufficient. As more products are developed within the same technology there may be cross-experience effects allowing further cost reduction.

There is only one situation when R&D unilaterally determines product specification in a development project. This happens after a successful quest for a new technology. Under these circumstances, the specifications of the first development project within the new technology will be R&D's responsibility. This success means that R&D will report on the availability of the technology, as well as on the completion of the first development project with its corresponding specifications. The project's name is also determined by R&D.

It is important to note that at least one year must elapse between the launch of a development project and its completion. This raises the need for an effective interface between marketing and R&D departments, allowing the former to recognize the latter's abilities and constraints. The lack of such awareness may lead to two types of problems.

1. Inability to launch or modify products on a timely basis.
2. Overspending on development projects because of time pressure.

Marketing should always be aware of what technologies are available for product development and keep a careful record of the successfully completed development projects. This will allow the use of such technical capabilities if a product must be launched at short notice. The investment necessary for a development project depends on its technological basis and the physical performance characteristics sought. The closer the specifications of a project are to a firm's successful development experience, the fewer funds that will be required. R&D will report on each active development project's status and required funds (see Figure 5-4). Exhibit 5-2 displays the minimum funds necessary for any development project for each of the technologies at the opening period. A useful strategy for development may be to allocate a small budget to a project so that R&D may do a feasibility study on it; that is, evaluate it both technically and economically and report back to marketing on the funds necessary for completion.

* R & D MESSAGES

* "FEASIBILITY" STUDY

* PAST EXPERIENCE
* COMPLETED PROJECTS
* TECHNOLOGY
* VARIOUS CHARACTERISTICS = DIFFERENT PROBLEMS
* UNCERTAINTY
* MINIMUM ACCORDING TO INDUSTRY EXPERTS

Figure 5-4 Product development—Budget specification

Messages from R&D on Development Projects

If a development project is not successful, one or more of the following self explanatory messages will be sent from R&D:

1. TECHNOLOGY FOR PROJECT (NAME) NOT AVAILABLE.

2. PROJECT (NAME) NOT FEASIBLE WITH SPECIFIED TECHNOLOGY.

3. BASE COST FOR PROJECT (NAME) TOO LOW. MINIMUM GUARAN-TEED FEASIBLE BASE COST IS $ (NUMBER) ADDITIONAL BUDGET REQUIRED $(NUMBER). IF YOU PURSUE THIS PROJECT, REMEMBER TO ADJUST BOTH BASE COST AND REQUIRED BUDGET FOR INFLA-TION.

4. ADDITIONAL BUDGET REQUIRED FOR COMPLETION OF BUDGET (NAME) $(NUMBER). IF YOU PURSUE THIS PROJECT, REMEMBER TO ADJUST REQUIRED BUDGET FOR INFLATION.

5. PROJECT (NAME) KEPT WITH ORIGINAL CHARACTERISTICS. IF CHANGES DESIRED IN CHARACTERISTICS 1 TO 4, LAUNCH AN-OTHER PROJECT WITH NEW NAME.

INTERFIRM COOPERATION

Although competition between INDUSTRAT firms is encouraged, cooperation in the form of licensing and joint venture arrangements is allowed as it helps to diffuse inno-vations and increase research efficiency. This section covers such activities, which are subject to the approval of the INDUSTRAT administration.

A licensing agreement may be negotiated between a firm which has completed a development project and another which has yet to complete such work but would like, nevertheless, to launch a product with such specifications. The licensee's justification in paying the fee is to take advantage of market opportunities. The licensor's motivation might be twofold: (1) to exploit an innovation beyond the market currently covered, and (2) to provide his own clients with an alternative source of supply. The second reason may help to increase the clients' commitment to a new product or technology.

An automatic fee of 3 percent of the sales revenues at list price will be made by the licensee to the licensor annually, and will be added to the licensor's contribution. The licensee and the licensor must base their negotiations on the development project and agree to a minimum annual payment. This fee is to compensate the licensor if sales do not reach the expected level, or if the licensee decides to discontinue the arrangement at a later date. Any other transfer of funds between firms will be handled by the game administrator. INDUSTRAT firms may use the licensing and fund transfer mechanism to enable further collaboration: if a competitor possesses a certain technology, another firm may ask that this competitor develop a particular product for eventual licensing (see Figure 5-5).

While development projects are transferable between firms, technologies are not. If one firm wishes to allow another to have access to a new technology, the arrangement must be implemented only through the licensing mechanism of the INDUSTRAT sim-ulation. If two firms agree to pool their resources and carry out technology research, the research will be performed in the facilites of one of the partners. This research will yield an automatic first development project, and all subsequent development and cost reduction projects which are subject to this agreement must be carried out only on the premises of the firm that performed the research. Proper care should be taken in the agreement to anticipate that an eventual demand for development capacity for both will be satisfied by the technological capacities possessed only by one side.

• NEGOTIATIONS	ONLY WITHIN APPROVED PERIODS
• OUTCOME	LICENSING AND / OR JOINT RESEARCH
• TERMS	NEGOTIATED FUND TRANSFERS DURING R&D NEGOTIATED MINIMUM FEE AFTER LAUNCH AUTOMATIC ROYALTIES (%)
• PROCESS	APPLICATION TO GAME ADMINISTRATOR
• IMPLEMENTATION	COMMON PROJECT NAMES AND PAYMENT TERMS FUND TRANSFERS VIA ADMINISTRATOR
• RISK	GOVERNMENT INVALIDATES CONTRACT IN VIEW OF COMPETITIVE CONDITIONS

Figure 5-5 Collaboration

Although this form of cooperation may be economically beneficial, such agreements may hamper competition in INDUSTRAT. Any licensing or fund transfer arrangement will require the approval of the government, represented by the simulation's administrator. Moreover, the government may unilaterally discontinue licensing arrangements that seriously restrict competition. The INDUSTRAT administration will announce when licensing negotiations are allowed and at what time period. All negotiations outside this specified time are illegal. INDUSTRAT teams may solicit the administrator for an announcement of the license negotiations period. Any licensing of development projects must be submitted by both parties to the game administrator. A failure to comply by either party will result in the inability to implement the agreement and a loss of the funds involved.

chapter 6

INDUSTRAT Procedures

In the INDUSTRAT simulation each team of participants represents one of five competing firms and makes annual operational decisions on its behalf. The directives given by the team are carried out through the year and the outcome will be known only after the year is over (see Figure 6-1). The execution of the annual plans is delegated to lower management, which operates autonomously during the year. In the case of an error by top management, lower management is accordingly restricted in the size of its adjustments.

Top management decisions are represented by the annual *decision form* submitted by each team. These decisions are examined for adherence to the simulation's rules and automatically adjusted if teams did not comply with the rules. For example, the total expenses a team incurs must not exceed the authorized expenditure budget. The adjustments consist of arbitrary cuts in the amounts that the teams had planned to spend on the year's operations. Any such decisions that are technically wrong will be detected and automatically replaced by technically correct decisions.

The set of market research studies monitoring the annual developments in the market place is available at any period. Each firm must order the studies it needs in advance of the year in question to be able to evaluate the year's developments. The annual decisions and market research orders are submitted through the decision form at the end of each decision session. If a firm needs market research information, but failed to order it in advance, the INDUSTRAT administration may impose higher prices on studies not ordered in advance.

In addition to the decision form, two other documents are provided: one for annual budgeting and the other for long range strategic planning. Both are designed in a format which facilitates the handling of internal budgeting and planning issues and, if required, are to be submitted to the INDUSTRAT administrator.

At the beginning of the game, each team receives the company report for the opening period, Period 0, giving the initial situation (the inheritance from the previous management). This makes up the groups' information for the first session, with which they complete their decision forms for the first year of managing the firms. The company report for this year, or period, will be handed out at the beginning of the next decision

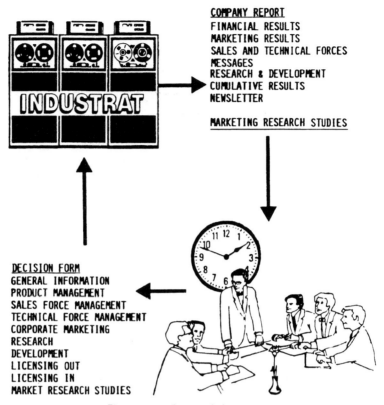

Figure 6-1 External documents

session. Then the team will evaluate the results of their first year and prepare the directives to be executed the year after.

THE COMPANY REPORT

The company report is divided into the following parts:

1. Financial results
2. Marketing results
3. Sales and technical forces
4. Messages
5. Research and development
6. Cumulative results
7. Newsletter

Appendix A presents a specimen company report. Since the competitive dynamics of each run of INDUSTRAT are different, this report is only to be used as an example. We refer to this report to familiarize the reader with the information received during the course of the simulation.

Financial Results

In Section 1, a detailed account is given of each product's performance, ending with the product's gross marketing contribution. Expense items, which were not allocated to individual products, are then subtracted from the total gross marketing contribution, yielding the net marketing contribution for the period.

The first group of figures in each column represents the annual volume of *production*, the volume of *units sold*, and excess *inventory* left at the year'a end. The volume of production is a function of what had been requested by marketing, automatically adjustable upward or downward by a maximum of 20 percent in view of the actual demand. If the product shows excess inventory at the end of the year, an over-optimistic sales forecast is suggested. Excess inventory also suggests that the maximum downward adjustment of 20 percent was made, but did not suffice to leave the firm without any inventory. On the other hand, when there is no excess inventory, comparison with the production request for the period may tell us the extent of the adjustment. If the full adjustment of 20 percent upward was employed, market research information must be used to estimate the level of actual market demand and lost sales due to the stock-out.

Marketing does not pay the production department for the manufacture of excess inventory, but it will do so upon sale, or if it is written off as obsolete. The costs of manufacture of the discarded inventory will automatically appear negatively in the entry *Exceptional Costs or Profit* unless sold to a third party, represented by the simulation administrator (see Figure 6-2).

The next two lines represent pricing information for each product. *List price* represents the pricing policy adopted by the firm for the year. The *average price* represents the actual prices obtained by the sales force in the field. The difference between list and average price is the aggregate discount given by the sales force to their customers. The maximum of any discount has been determined by marketing in the decision form.

The next group of figures represents the cost structure per unit, which is composed of the manufacturing, licensing, and commission costs per unit. *Unit manufacturing costs* are the result of three factors, manufacturing methods, experience effects, and inflationary effects. Manufacturing methods in INDUSTRAT are represented by the base cost, the average cost for the first 100,000 units produced. Experience effects result from efforts to reduce costs. These would usually decrease with experience. The effects of inflation vary according to the annual inflation rate. As long as the production department employs the same production method (the same base cost), marketing may utilize the past behavior

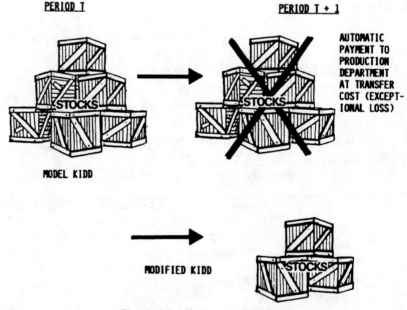

Figure 6-2 Brand modification

of production costs and forecasted inflation to estimate the next and subsequent year's unit manufacturing costs.

Unit licensing cost represents the automatic licensing payment of 3 percent of list price paid to the licensor of the product. This cost item appears as soon as a licensing agreement enters into effect and disappears automatically if the product is either eliminated from the line or modified through an internal development project. *Unit commission* represents the incentive received by the sales force for each unit sold. It corresponds to the percentage commission authorized by marketing and applies to the average price obtained for this product in the field.

The next group of figures represents *sales revenue* and the costs to be subtracted from it. The number of units sold is multiplied by the average price to provide the sales revenue. Unit costs for licensing and sales commissions are also multiplied by units sold to provide their corresponding totals. Next come the product's expenditures for its own promotion, advertising and technical support. These figures also correspond to the decisions made prior to the year's start. The final cost item is the *inventory holding costs* for the product. It is calculated by applying the official inventory holding cost rate to the value of the excess inventory. The rate is published annually in the newsletter. The final figure in each column is the resulting *gross marketing contribution* for the product.

Global Results. The previous results, aggregated across the individual products, yield the *total gross marketing contribution*. At this point, one may subtract the expenditure items, not allocated to products. These items are the sales force's fixed costs (hiring, firing, and employment), their training, corporate communication. research for new technology, product development, and market research. The balance is the year's *operational marketing contribution*.

This figure is then adjusted by adding the revenues from licensing development projects to other companies and including any exceptional profits or losses. Losses are the consequence of insufficient minimum annual royalty payments, payments for obsolete inventory to production, or other adjustments by the simulation administrator. The result yields the firm's *net marketing contribution*.

The final figure in the financial results is the *marketing expenditure budget* authorized for the next year of operations. The size of this budget is a fraction of the net marketing contribution achieved and will be devoted to marketing. The balance will be used for capital investments and dividends elsewhere. As the contribution rises, the size of the marketing expenditure budget should normally increase. However, it should not be expected to grow at the same rate as the net marketing contribution. The reason is that beyond a certain threshold the marginal effectiveness of marketing expenditure diminishes, and so the fraction for next year's budget will diminish as well. In fact, beyond a certain size of net marketing contribution the absolute size of next year's marketing expenditure budget will stay at the same level. On the other hand, a minimum budget for marketing expenditure will be unilaterally provided when the net marketing contribution is too low.

Marketing

Section 2 reports on each product's performance. The market is divided into three submarkets, testing, supplementary, and major sources of supply, each representing a stage of product adoption by accounts. The product's performance is first expressed by its share in each submarket.

The sales in clients' tests are very small and insignificant with respect to unit volume and monetary value. Comparison of value and unit volume shares for the supplementary and major source submarkets is provided. The shares in the two submarkets, supplementary and primary, are presented first in terms of unit volume and subsequently in terms of monetary values.

There may be instances when the marketing report displays a product as a supplementary source with a market share larger than 100 percent. This happens because some clients in the market maintain policies of multiple sourcing. When there is insufficient supply, a client will return to his supplier for another transaction. These separate transactions may satisfy the clients' policies for the remainder of the year but will result in computations of shares larger than 100 percent. This demonstrates the existence of opportunities for more suppliers.

Sales and Technical Forces

Section 3 shows the sizes and organizational structures of the sales and technical support forces deployed by the company in the field. The first part of this section provides the organizational structure. This structure follows one of the three macrosegmentation criteria, geography, account size, or end product.

The proportion displayed in the row of the macrosegmentation scheme chosen as organizational structure represents the allocation of salespersons assigned to each of these macrosegments. The proportions in the other rows represent the way individual salespersons spent their time between the segments, according to each scheme. Although the decision on their allocation of assignments is up to the sales and technical support departments, they try to conform to marketing's decisions. The resulting allocation of salespersons' and technicians' time is displayed for each segmentation scheme.

Messages

Section 4 points out technical or administrative errors detected and automatically corrected during the simulation. For example, such an incident may occur when the teams' decisions require an expenditure budget greater than the one authorized. An INDUSTRAT policy determining budgetary items to be cut, in cases of erroneously excessive budgets, is built into the simulation. The unauthorized budgetary excess will be eliminated by sequentially subtracting the unauthorized excesses from certain budget elements. The sequence of these elements is arbitrary. If, following one subtraction, there still remains an excess, all or part of another budgetary item will be subtracted. This process will continue until the expenditure budget conforms to the original allocation. The sequence of budgetary items to be cut in such cases remains the same throughout the simulation. When such cuts are performed, the message will identify the budget items that were affected. As the assumption is that such errors are not malicious, the cuts will avoid items of strategic long run consequence, unless the total excess is not covered otherwise.

Competing teams are encouraged to verify their arithmetic before submitting the decisions. Normally the administrator will not have the time to contact a team if an error is detected. On the other hand, teams may try to renegotiate their expenditure budgets with the administrator. To do so, they must present a coherent and defensible plan. In any case, they may not be in a position to do so until well into the simulation.

Research and Development

Each year the company report provides a status report on all projects, completed and in progress, in the R&D department. Successful research allows the firm to launch product development projects based on the newly acquired technology. This in turn permits the launching of products with new specifications, modification of present ones, and cost reduction via changed production methods. If projects have not been completed, the R&D department will monitor funds already spent, and provide information on the resources necessary for completion.

Research. Each column in Section 5A is a status report of a single technology. The first four columns refer to Korex technologies 1, 2, 3, and 4, respectively. The last column relates to technology 5, Lomex products. The first row shows the investment accumulated during the simulation for each of these technologies.

Each technology requires an annual minimum of dedicated resources, giving it the critical mass for the necessary progress. The minimum number of years necessary for the completion of the research was listed, for each technology, in Exhibit 5-2 (page 34). The second row of the report on research monitors the number of years for which research investment was allocated in this fashion. If for a given technology there has been investment, but never at an annual amount above the neccessary critical mass, the first row will show the cumulative investment and the second row will show 0, implying that although research has been done, the minimum number of years listed in Exhibit 5-2 must still be spent.

The third row reports the status of access to the technology. If a NO appears, no development of products may be undertaken as yet within this technology. If, for a given column, the entry in this row is OK, the firm may proceed with development projects using this technology for eventual product modification and introduction. In fact, in the year the search for a given technology is complete, the first development project will be successfully concluded and reported in the development section given next. The specifications of this project are within the range of the newly available technology and were determined by technical considerations in the research team.

The investment allocation necessary during the research period is shown in the last three rows of this table. *Minimum total investment* represents the resources without which concluding the research would be impossible. The entry updates the information in Exhibit 5-2, which applies to the starting point of the simulation. *Proposed total investment* is the research department's estimation of the amount at which attaining the technology is practically guaranteed. The difference between the two amounts represents the uncertainties involved in the quest for the technology. Naturally, the decision whether to spend an amount close to the minimum, the proposed, or somewhere in between rests with the marketing department. It reflects the marketing department's sense of urgency, available resources, and willingness to undertake risk.

Finally, the *minimum annual investment,* representing a critical mass allowing one year's progress, is updated in the last row. While Exhibit 5.2 shows what this amount is at the opening stage of the simulation, there is a need to consider inflation and other factors that make this threshold change from year to year. An annual investment, smaller than this minimum, would reduce the additional investment required but it would not shorten the duration of the search for the technology. Careful consideration of the annual minima should prevent a firm from making an investment without having attained access to the technology.

Development. Section 5B provides a cumulative update on all product development projects and their status. Each column represents a project that was assigned to a development group in R&D. The identity of each project has been coded by the initiators using the INDUSTRAT name convention. The report first shows the technology base, the cumulative investment to date, and whether the project has been completed. An OK in the row representing project status allows the firm to exploit this development in the coming year as a new or modified product. A NO implies that investment in this development project must continue before it can be completed. The rest of the chart repeats the specifications of the product under development, with four rows representing physical characteristics of the product sought. The last row represents the base production costs specified by marketing and is continually updated for inflation.

The remainder of the development report indicates what is required to complete unfinished projects. For each incomplete project, a message will appear specifying the remaining investment necessary for completion. No minimum time prerequisite is necessary here. Sufficient funds may accelerate a development project.

Any continued development project must respect the information and messages already displayed in the development report. These messages cover problems of technological availability, project name changes, unrealistic base costs, budgetary corrections for inflation, and other incidents requiring attention. Lack of attention to such details causes delays in product development that might eventually handicap the firm. Teams are encouraged to request the assistance of the INDUSTRAT administrator in case of doubt.

Cumulative Results

This section presents the cumulative results achieved by the firm since the start of the simulation. The first and second rows represent the periods in which each product was introduced and last modified, respectively. When the entries in these two rows are equal for a given product, the implication is that it has not been modified since its introduction. The remainder of this section of the company report provides a cumulative view structured similarly to the annual financial results.

Newsletter

The newsletter (Section 7 of the sample report) is a source of information, generally well known to the industry by the end of the year. It first lists several environmental factors, such as GNP growth and inflation rates for this year and those expected for next year. It then displays a series of cost factors that every firm needs to consider in the preparation of the expense budget for the next period: the salaries, hiring, and firing costs of sales persons and technicians. Note that a new salesperson incurs both hiring costs and a salary in the first year of employment.

The cost of each of the market research studies is announced in the newsletter and is updated annually. The final published factor is the cost of holding inventory. This will determine, for a given value of excess inventory, the holding costs for the next period.

The third part of the newsletter is devoted to specific messages and newsflashes which may be sent to the firm from the administration of the INDUSTRAT simulation. These messages, unlike the ones in the messages section above, are entered manually by the administrators. The message may be a broadcast to all teams, in which case it appears as a *Newsflash*, or it may be a private message to the firm. The latter appears under *Specific message to . . .* and will appear only on the given team's report. The messages may also originate from other teams, in which case the administrator only relays the message according to the wishes of the firm broadcasting it.

The fourth part of the newsletter provides information about the launching and modification of products on the market by all firms. For each product launched or modified, the physical characteristics to date and the base cost are displayed together with the first year's list price. The final part of the newsletter provides sales, list prices, and market share information for every product currently available on the market.

THE DECISION FORM

This document is used by each INDUSTRAT team to communicate its annual decisions. An example is presented in Exhibit 6-1. The first group of entries is used for administrative purposes. Each figure entered here prepares the simulation to consider the decisions submitted later in the decision form. The team must indicate its identity, the number of products it will offer, development projects to be continued or initiated, and the number of licensing relationships to be started.

If several INDUSTRAT simulations are run in parallel, each is an independent industry containing five competitors. The identity of each firm within its industry is identified by the numbers 1 through 5, and the identity of the industry by one letter of the alphabet. The remainder of the decision form provides the following details of the various marketing decisions to be entered:

1. Product management
2. Sales force management
3. Technical force management
4. Corporate marketing
5. Research and development
6. Licensing operations
7. Market research studies
8. Administrative adjustments

Product Management

The number of rows completed in this section must correspond to the figure previously entered for the number of products offered. The first column contains the name of the product, conforming to the INDUSTRAT conventions: the first letter either K for Korex or L for Lomex. The second letter is A, E, I, O, or U according to the firm's identity (1, 2, 3, 4, or 5, respectively). The last two letters are uniquely determined by the firm. Product names may be retained while changing specifications via the use of development projects, which constitutes a product modification. A firm may not carry more than one product with the same name, although products with different names may be identical in the four physical specifications, and may even be derived from one common development project (note that we deal only with the four most important physical specifications; other characteristics may indeed be different according to decisions made at lower levels of management). However, once a product name is removed from the line, it may never be introduced again in the course of the simulation, since the market will have perceived it as a failure. The erroneous introduction of such an obsolete product name would be signaled with a message. There would be no other negative effects on the firm's image in the market place, as the removal of a product from the line entails an automatic loss of awareness for the product.

A series of specific decisions is entered following the name of the product in each row. If the name of the product is followed by a blank in the column titled Development Project, there is no change in any of the four physical characteristics of the product. Production would continue according to last year's specifications. On the other hand, a change in specifications is implemented by entering the name of a development project that has been successfully completed by the development department. Note that the development department must first report the successful completion of the project before the results may be used for product modification, which necessarily introduces a delay of at least one year. This procedure is applicable to cost reduction projects as well as to the introduction of new products.

The firm is free to use any development project for product introduction and modification, provided that the project has been successfully completed by the development department. A successful Korex development project may be used immediately or in any later year to modify or reduce base cost, or to introduce a Korex product. The same project may be reused if specifications have been replaced. Furthermore, the same project

INDUSTRAT DECISION FORM

Firm: **3**

Number of products for sale: **6**

Number of development projects: **2**

Number of new projects licensed out: **0**

Number of new projects licensed in: **0**

Industry: **A**

Period: **5**

PRODUCT MANAGEMENT

	Product Name	Development Project (New/Mod Product Only)	Production ('000s)	List Price ($)	Maximum Price Discount (%)	Sales Force Commission (%)	Promotion ($'000)	Product Advertising ($'000)	Allocation of Technical Support (%)
2	LIFE	PLIA	100	200	10	7	600	600	30
3	KILT		17	390	5	5	75	10	8
4	KILL		3	440	5	5	100	100	10
5	KISS	PKISU	18	500	5	5	200	100	10
6	KIDU		27	525	10	5	200	100	22
7	KINE	PKIND	83	520	5	5	300	100	20
8									
9									
10									
11									100 %

SALES FORCE MANAGEMENT

12 Organizational Structure (code): **3** Total Number of Salespersons: **79** Sales Force Training ($'000): **200**

ALLOCATION (%)

13 Geography: E **30** C **40** W **30** 100 %

14 Size: S **34** M **33** L **33** 100 %

15 End Product: I **10** CN **40** CR **50** 100 %

16 DMU: P **30** E **24** PU **29** G **18** 100 %

TECHNICAL FORCE MANAGEMENT

17 Total Number of Technicians: **40** Tech Force Training ($'000): **150**

ALLOCATION (%)

18 Geography: E **30** C **40** W **30** 100 %

19 Size: S **34** M **33** L **33** 100 %

20 End Product: I **10** CN **40** CR **50** 100 %

21 DMU: P **45** E **45** PU **5** G **5** 100 %

CORPORATE MARKETING

22 Corporate Communications ($'000): **100**

RESEARCH AND DEVELOPMENT

Research

	Technology (Code)	Investment ($'000)
23	0	0

Development

	Project Name (P)	Technology (Code)	Budget ($'000)	Physical Characteristics 1	2	3	4	Base Cost ($)
24	PLICK	5	650	20	100	50	500	68
25	PLIA	5	5	17	101	43	224	50
26								
27								

NEW LICENSING OUT

	Project Name (P)	To Firm (N*)	Minimum Annual Fee ($'000)
29			
30			
31			
32			
33			

NEW LICENSING IN

	Project Name (P ...)	From Firm (N*)	Minimum Annual Fee ($'000)
34			
35			

MARKET RESEARCH STUDIES (Codes)

1	2	3	4	5	6	7	8	9	10	11	12	13	14	15	16
2	2	2	2	2	2	2	2	2	2	2	2	2	2	2	2

ADMINISTRATIVE ADJUSTMENTS ($'000)

36 **1709** **2000**

EC (−) EP (+)   BD (−) BI (+)

Exhibit 6-1

48

MODIFICATIONS RESULTING FROM NEGOTIATIONS BETWEEN
THE FIRM AND THE GAME ADMINISTRATOR

Source of Modification	Exceptional Profits (+) or Costs (—) ($'000)	Budget Increase (+) or Decrease (—) ($'000)
1. Additional information bought from the game administrator		
2. Payment to the Production Department by INDUSTRAT administration for liquidation of obsolete inventory		
3. Changes in Marketing Expenditure Budget		
4. Fines		
5. Other Modifications		
TOTAL		

Under section 2:

Brand x Quantity ('000) x Manufac- turing Cost x Proportion (%)

Signature of the firm's representative _____

Signature of the game administrator _____

Exhibit 6-1 (continued)

name may be used simultaneously with more than one Korex product. The procedure is identical for Lomex products. Finally, Korex and Lomex may not be mixed on the same row. Any expenses dedicated to such a product would be lost.

Next in this section, the marketing department specifies the requested production level, the official list price, maximum percentage price discount that salespersons are authorized to give, the commission rate received by salespersons, and the promotional and advertising expenses for this product. The last column represents the percentage of the technical support package allocated to the product in the given row. (The technical support budget as a whole is discussed shortly under Technical Force Management). These percentages must total to 100 percent across all the products offered.

Sales Force Management

All salespersons in INDUSTRAT may sell any product offered by their firms. Salespersons are allocated to the different accounts by market segments, which in this simulation may be defined by geographical regions, different potential account sizes, or by the types of product involved. Since an allocation of salespersons according to more than one segmentation criterion at a time is not practical, the marketing department must specify one priority criterion as a basis for sales force organization. Marketing may only suggest the proportion of overall sales force contact time to be devoted to market segments defined according to the other criteria.

The sales department allocates salespersons to segments according to marketing's segmentation criteria for sales force organization. The allocation of sales effort defined by the other segmentation criteria will guide individual salespersons within their segments The macrosegmentation criteria geography, account size, and end product are coded 1, 2, and 3, respectively. After placing one of these numbers in the box organizational structure, the department will use the corresponding criterion for salesperson segment assignments.

The second and third boxes in the top row relate to the total number of salespersons and the sales force training budget, respectively. The former figure will be used, together with the fixed cost per salesperson as published in the newsletter, to compute the sales force payroll. If the total number of salespersons is larger than the one in the previous period, the difference is multiplied by the cost of hiring a new salesperson. If the number of salespersons is smaller than in the last period, the difference is multiplied by the cost of firing a salesperson. Both the hiring and firing costs are also published in the newsletter annually, and their totals are added to the sales force costs.

The last part of the sales force management section is devoted to the detailed allocation of sales force contact time to the various segments. A percentage allocation is required for each macro and microsegmentation criterion, adding up to 100 percent for each row. One of the three macrosegmentation criteria would have been chosen in the organizational structure earlier in this section. This allocation is implemented in full through the assignation of salespersons to segments. The others serve as guidelines for each salesperson.

Technical Force Management

The structure of the decisions in this section is similar to that of the sales force section. First, the number of technicians employed should be indicated on the decision form. This number is then automatically multiplied by the annual cost per technician to determine the payroll for the force. The difference between the sizes of the technical forces for this year and for the last are in turn multiplied by the hiring or the firing cost, whichever is appropriate, and added to the payroll. The next item in the technical support budget is the training of the technical force.

The remainder of this section is devoted to guidelines on the allocation of the technical support resources. For each segmentation scheme, a proportion per segment should be entered, adding up to 100 percent across each row. As in the sales force section, it may be difficult to follow all segmentation schemes simultaneously. Moreover, the technical force is also allocated across products in the product management section. The priority here will follow the organizational scheme used for the sales force, with all other allocations serving as guidelines. Similarly, the more training a technician receives, the closer he or she will be able to adhere to marketing's directives.

Corporate Marketing

This part of the decision form contains the amount allocated for corporate communications. Recall that this expenditure is neither product nor segment specific. It is devoted to promoting the organization as a whole in the marketplace.

Research and Development

This section of the decision form is divided into research and development parts. In the research part, the four Korex technologies are designated by 1, 2, 3, and 4, respectively, and the Lomex technology by the code 5. Each year the R&D department may be instructed to allocate resources to help provide the firm with one of the five technologies. The code for this technology is entered in this section of the decision form together with the budget devoted to this purpose.

A technology search requires a minimum investment and number of years to be completed. Note that technological research may be pursued for only one technology in a given year. The choice of the annual technology investment represents a major commitment in both terms of expenses and lost time in the case of a wrong choice.

The development section includes product development projects designed for the future launch of new products or product changes. The firm may enter up to four projects in this space. For each project the form must include a project name as specified in the INDUSTRAT name convention, and the technology on which it will be based. Only technologies already possessed by the firm are acceptable in this section. Projects based on technologies not available to the firm are automatically to be rejected and their corresponding budgets wasted.

The remainder of the entry line for each project includes the annual development budget, the project's physical specifications, and production base costs. The physical characteristics must be within feasible ranges of the corresponding technology. Any specification outside these ranges will cause a loss of the budget devoted to the wrongly specified project. Continued development projects must carry the same name as in the past, with no change in specifications. Any change in one of the four physical specifications will be ignored by the simulation. However, changes in base costs while a development project is in progress are permitted.

It must be emphasized that the result of any development project may not be used until the development department has signaled a successful completion. Once this is achieved, the desired product modification, cost reduction, or new product launch is implemented if, and only if, the successful project name is entered in the second column of the product management section, following the desired product.

Licensing Operations

This section implements new collaboration agreements between INDUSTRAT firms. The first part lists the new agreement in which the firm is the licensor, whereas the second lists those in which the firm is a new licencee. A project name, a number designating the identity of the collaborating firm, and the annual minimum payment agreed upon are listed for every agreement approved by the simulation administrator. A maximum of five

INDUSTRAT BUDGETING FORM

Industry _____

Firm _____

Period _____

										TOTALS	
Product Name											
Production ('000 Units)											
Quantity Sold ('000 Units)											
Inventory ('000 Units)											
List Price ($)											
Average Price ($)											
Unit Manufacturing Costs ($)											
Unit Licensing Costs ($)											
Unit Commissions ($)											
Total Unit Costs											
Revenue from Sales ($'000)											
Manufacturing Costs ($'000)											
Licensing Costs ($'000)											
Sales Commission ($'000)											Prom.
Promotion ($'000)											Pr Adv.
Product Advertising ($'000)											Tech.
Technical Support * ($'000)											
Inventory Holding Costs ($'000)											
Gross Marketing Contribution ($'000)										TOTAL	
Fixed Sales Force Costs ($'000)											
Sales Force Training Costs ($'000)											
Corporate Communication ($'000)											
Research ($'000)											
Development ($'000)											
Market Research ($'000)											
Total Marketing Expenditures											
Operational Marketing Contribution ($'000)											
Revenue from Licensing ($'000)											
Exceptional Costs or Profits ($'000)											
Net Marketing Contribution ($'000)											

* (Total package of technical support) x (proportion allocated to the individual product, as per decision form)

Exhibit 6-2

SALES FORECAST INPUT FOR BUDGETING

PRODUCT	AGGREGATE	MACROSEGMENTATION SCHEME CHOSEN *									UNIT SALES
		REGIONS			ACCOUNT POTENTIAL			END USE			
		EAST	CENTRAL	WEST	SMALL	MEDIUM	LARGE	COMM.	INST.	CONS.	
KOREX MARKET FORECAST ('000 UNITS)											
LOMEX MARKET FORECAST ** ('000 UNITS)											

1											
2											
3											
4											
5											
6											
7											
8											
9											
10											

* Please use only the columns applicable to the macrosegmentation scheme (if you choose).

** You may apply your expected shares in segment/market to compute your corresponding sales forecasts.

Exhibit 6-2 INDUSTRAT Budgeting Form (reverse side)

agreements may be reached annually on new licensing out whereas a maximum of two may be reached on new licensing in agreements. Any discrepancy in the details of a licensing agreement as displayed in the licencee's and the licensor's decision forms will prevent the implementation of a licensing agreement. Licensing arrangements are automatically maintained once initiated. Therefore it is not necessary to resubmit this information for the following years.

Market Research

Each of the sixteen market research studies available in the INDUSTRAT simulation may be ordered in this section of the form. The firm may designate in the corresponding box the macrosegmentation criterion for which the information is displayed. The code 1 indicates aggregate information only with no segmentation requested. The codes 2, 3, and 4 specify that in addition to aggregate information, the firm would like to have the study results communicated by one of the macrosegmentation criteria—geography, account size, or end product, respectively. The code 5 indicates that the market research firm should supply the segmentation criterion for which the differences between the segments are the greatest.

The code 0 or a blank box will represent a lack of interest on the firm's part to purchase the corresponding study. Note that to order a study, one should mark the corresponding box and that the codes 1 to 5 will incur a cost per study based on the basic price, multiplied by an appropriate factor. The basic price published in the newsletter refers to the code 1. The multiplying factor, for codes 2–4, will be 1.5 for each of the macrosegmentation and 2.0 for statistically optimal segmentation criteria.

Administrative Adjustments

This part of the decision form should be left empty as it is used by the INDUSTRAT administration for adjustments. They should be identical to the bottom line of the reverse side of the decision form (see Exhibit 6-1), in which various arrangements, negotiated with the firm, are recorded. Because of the variety of such arrangements, there is sometimes a need to record them manually.

For example, investment in research for new technologies is relatively expensive

RESEARCH & DEVELOPMENT	PRICING	SALESFORCE	TECHNICAL SUPPORT
TECHNOLOGY PRODUCT DEVELOPMENT COST REDUCTION	PRICE LIST MAXIMUM DISCOUNT AUTHORIZED	SIZE DEPLOYMENT ORGANIZATION COMMISSION STRUCTURE TRAINING	SIZE DEPLOYMENT TRAINING
COMMUNICATION	COLLABORATION	ANTITRUST REGULATION	MARKET RESEARCH
PROMOTION PRODUCT ADVERTISING CORPORATE COMMUNICATION	LICENSING JOINT RESEARCH	INTERFIRM CONTRACT APPROVAL PRICE CONTROLS GOVERNMENT INTERVENTION	16 STUDIES PRESPECIFIED SEGMENTS

Figure 6-3   Annual decisions of the INDUSTRAT firm

INDUSTRAT STRATEGIC PLANNING FORM

_____
_____
_____
_____
_____
_____
_____
_____
_____
_____
_____
_____
_____
_____
_____
_____
_____
_____
_____
_____
_____
_____
_____
_____

Exhibit 6-3 (Front side)

FORECAST RESULTING FROM STRATEGIC PLANNING

Firm_____   Industry_____

GENERAL PERFORMANCE		1	2	3	4	5	6	7	8	9	10
Market Share (%) of $ Sales	Objective										
	Outcome										
Sales Revenue ($'000)	Objective										
	Outcome										
Manufacturing Costs ($'000)	Objective										
	Outcome										
Sales Commission ($'000)	Objective										
	Outcome										

PRODUCT MARKETING EXPENDITURES

Promotion ($'000)	Objective										
	Outcome										
Product Advertising ($'000)	Objective										
	Outcome										
Technical Support ($'000)	Objective										
	Outcome										
Licensing Costs ($'000)	Objective										
	Outcome										

UNALLOCATED MARKETING EXPENDITURES

Fixed Sales Force Costs ($'000)	Objective										
	Outcome										
Sales Force Training Costs ($'000)	Objective										
	Outcome										
Corporate Communication ($'000)	Objective										
	Outcome										
Research ($'000)	Objective										
	Outcome										
Development ($'000)	Objective										
	Outcome										
Market Research ($'000)	Objective										
	Outcome										
Total Marketing Expenditures ($'000)	Objective										
	Outcome										
Operational Contribution ($'000)	Objective										
	Outcome										
Licensing Revenues ($'000)	Objective										
	Outcome										

Net Marketing Contribution ($'000)	Objective										
	Outcome										
Others ($'000)	Objective										
	Outcome										

Exhibit 6-3 (reverse side)

and a firm may negotiate an increase in the expenditure budget for this purpose. Financing this increase may entail a long term loan from the INDUSTRAT bank (represented by the administrator), a grant, or a transfer of funds from another team. This transaction must be recorded to enable the firm to spend more than the amount authorized in the original expenditure budget for the next year. Similarly, the repayment of loans, sale of additional information, buying out of obsolete inventories, fines, and any other modifications must be duly recorded and totaled on the back of the decision form.

E BUDGETING FORM

The objective of the budgeting form, shown in Exhibit 6-2, is to systematically specify the company's use of its marketing budget and to estimate the net marketing contribution that may result from the firm's annual decisions (see Figure 6-3) in the current period. The budgeting form has the same structure as the first section of the company report and allows checking *a posteriori* for variations between a selected annual plan and the actual outcome. Obviously, the crucial estimates in the budgeting process concern the forecasted sales for each brand. The table on the reverse of the budgeting form should help formulate these forecasts in terms of market sizes and market shares in each segment. The computations to be performed in the budgeting process are straightforward. This is essentially an internal marketing department form, and is not submitted to the administrator unless specifically requested.

E PLANNING FORM

On this form, shown in Exhibit 6-3, the firm should specify the main strategic directions on which the plan is based. The reverse side of the planning form is designed to formalize quantifiable objectives and to provide a basis for the appraisal of a company's performance over successive simulated INDUSTRAT years. This form should be analyzed and updated

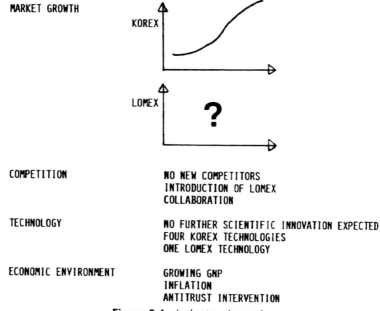

Figure 6-4   Industry dynamics

each period according to the company's evolution and the expected industry dynamics (see Figure 6-4). Although it is primarily for internal use, planning information may be requested at any time by the administrator. Successive plans realized in the course of the simulation will help the firm to evaluate and present its activities at the end of the simulation.

chapter 7

Some Suggestions Before You Start

Having read the INDUSTRAT manual, you have completed the initial preparation for the simulation. Managing an INDUSTRAT firm in competition with other teams is a challenging exercise, requiring familiarity with the administrative aspects of the simulation. The sooner the practical part of the simulation is understood, the earlier you can concentrate on the strategic issues (see Figure 7-1). This last section attempts to answer several questions, which, in the authors' experience, teams may have at this point. These questions are (1) How do we handle the first decision? (2) How should our team be organized? (3) What is the best strategy? (4) What is the role of the simulation administrator? and (5) How do we get the most out of this exercise?

YOUR FIRST DECISION

The simulation will start after your INDUSTRAT administrator has assigned you to your team and given out the first company report. You will learn that your firm is currently offering four products on the market, as are the four other competitors. Your initial report does not include any market research studies, since your predecessors did not order any. However, you may order studies for the next year, which, after analysis, will help to clarify the relative strengths and weaknesses of your firm.

For the first three years, it is recommended that the choice of organizational and macrosegmentation scheme follow the structure of your sales force for the previous year. This structure presumably follows a past macrosegmentation decision made by your predecessors. Because the volume of the market research information in this simulation is potentially enormous, your team should avoid buying too much information in the early stages of the simulation.

You should be conservative in your initial moves and not take any significant risks until more market intelligence is available. For example, you should not undertake any R&D projects designed to change your products' physical characteristics, or introduce

- LONG TERM PERSPECTIVE
- MARKETING AS A PROFIT CENTER
- MARKETING STRATEGY BASED ON SEGMENTATION, POSITIONING AND PORTFOLIO APPROACH
- MARKETING MIX DECISIONS SECONDARY TO STRATEGIC DECISIONS
- COMPETITIVE ENVIRONMENT

&

- PRODUCT / NON PRODUCT NEEDS
- CHOICE OF MACROSEGMENTATION SCHEMES
- MICROSEGMENTATION - DMU CONCEPT
- INDUSTRIAL ADOPTION PROCESS
- CORPORATE COMMUNICATION
- SALESFORCE MANAGEMENT
- TECHNICAL SUPPORT
- DISTINCTION BETWEEN RESEARCH AND DEVELOPMENT
- LICENSING AND JOINT VENTURES
- MARKET SEGMENTATION RESEARCH

Figure 7-1   INDUSTRAT features

new ones, until you are aware of the needs of the market and the way in which they evolve. Similarly, for lack of information, you should not yet attempt to reorganize the sales and the technical forces.

Your firm will not be able to introduce products with new physical characteristics until the necessary R&D is successfully completed. You should spend most of the time allotted for the first decision analyzing the way your predecessors allocated their resources. It is suggested that you formulate specific hypotheses on why they wanted to do it that way and test the hypotheses through market research studies. These will be available when the next company report is handed to your team. Blank forms for the entry of your group's annual decisions, as well as for the internal budgeting and planning, are provided in Appendix C.

TEAM ORGANIZATION

As in any complex business situation, the question of organization will soon arise. You should keep in mind that, as a participant in INDUSTRAT, you have two major objectives. On the one hand, you are a member of a team under time pressure in an increasingly complex competitive situation. In this role you will want your team to perform better than the competition, and that may require a certain division of tasks and responsibilities as the simulation grows more complex. On the other hand, as an individual you are participating in an educational exercise. In this context your personal objective is to learn as much as possible, which implies exposure to the different aspects of INDUSTRAT. While it is up to each group to organize itself in the way it sees fit, you will find that INDUSTRAT is designed to expose you to most aspects early on.

The outset of the INDUSTRAT competitive structure is designed to make your introduction to the simulation as smooth as possible. With only four Korex products offered, each team member will quickly contribute his or her initial observations, based on the information in this manual and the first company report. In the authors' experience, the variety of personal backgrounds represented in the team leads to a diversity in perception and will result in trading of information. As the simulation evolves and becomes more complex, each member of the team will be naturally inclined to make different contributions. Some groups will then formalize the different tasks of their members, whereas others will elect to continue the informal working environment.

NO OPTIMAL STRATEGY

In INDUSTRAT, as in many other business situations, the evolution of the market is subject to external and internal developments. While external forces are beyond the firms' control, strategic choices made by the INDUSTRAT firms will determine, to a large extent, the fate of the industry. It would be a mistake to try and guess what the single best strategy is, for the simple reason that there is no such strategy. The INDUSTRAT simulation is realistic in the sense that creativity may yield various successful strategies for a given competitive scenario. Moreover, certain strategies in one running of the simulation may well bring about quite different results in another, as the choices that competitors make rarely coincide.

Nevertheless, success in INDUSTRAT, as in other business situations, is not a result of random choice. Rigorous analysis, planning, and calculated risk taking will increase the likelihood of a good strategic choice. That, coupled with team spirit, will make the exercise more rewarding.

THE INDUSTRAT ADMINISTRATOR

The INDUSTRAT administrator does not manipulate the simulation during its running. Since there will be no intervention for or against any of the firms, your team will take sole responsibility for its performance. The administrator fills many roles during the simulation. He or she will act as instructor, corporate chief executive officer, market research supplier, banker, and manager of an export firm to whom your team can sell liquidated inventory. The administrator will also act as a superior authority, such as arbitrator, or government official, for cases of industrial espionage, collusion, or any other practices which in his or her opinion may be unethical or hamper competition.

The INDUSTRAT administrator must follow a tight timetable and supervise adherence to the time schedules by all groups. In order to facilitate this, the administrator may impose fines for late submission of forms. The fine system will be announced at the outset of the simulation. However, generally the game administrator will be reasonable, resourceful and ready to listen to well-documented reasoning in eventual negotiations.

GETTING THE MOST OUT OF THE INDUSTRAT SIMULATION

Here are several points of advice which will help to make the INDUSTRAT experience more valuable and enjoyable. INDUSTRAT is a strategic game, and as such, most of the analyses and discussions should be devoted to strategic issues. The short term aspects of INDUSTRAT are simplified to provide a strategic focus. Many are either performed automatically within the simulation or are not intended for your consideration.

The INDUSTRAT environment is quite complex, requiring caution before decisions are taken. As many factors operate simultaneously in the market, the explanations for certain events will require considerable research and discussions. What may be considered obvious at first glance may, in fact, appear quite differently following an in-depth analysis.

An abundant amount of information is available in this simulation. Its digestion could prove time consuming, and so, one must be selective in the way time is spent. It is possible to order all the annual research studies, but to digest them would take time. Each team will have to decide on the amount of information necessary to perform an analysis and still leave time for reasoned and steady decision making. One may want to postpone certain analyses and discussions until long term planning and staff work can be performed under less pressure. Similarly, when in a decision session, one should avoid lingering on minor issues at the expense of the major ones.

Administrative errors may occur due to incorrect completion of the forms or over a misunderstanding of certain rules. The INDUSTRAT administrator will make every effort to help avoid such errors. It is the team's responsibility to conform to the rules of the simulation. If in doubt, the team should refer to the administrator for assistance. A useful practice for every team is to appoint one member to be responsible for completing the various forms and to serve as liaison between the group and the administrator throughout the simulation.

A FINAL WORD

You are entering a simulation that provides a lot of information and opportunity for analysis. You will soon find that the wealth of information, while reducing uncertainty, will not replace judgement, intuition, and risk-taking ability. The INDUSTRAT information system will help formulate alternative courses of action, but in the final analysis the choice is yours. You will find that the simulation may either be a smooth or a rough experience, depending on the competitive circumstances. The dynamics of your team will play a major factor in the way your firm overcomes the challenges that await you.

The competitive setting necessarily implies that some firms will perform better than others. At the start of the INDUSTRAT simulation the stance of each of the five firms includes certain inherent competitive strengths and weaknesses. You should expect your firm's initial performance to be the result of this profile. However, the structure of the market may drastically change as a result of the firms' analysis, strategies, and quality of execution. Finally, as one would expect in an industrial environment, a certain element of random luck, in terms of creative ideas and timing of actions, may intervene.

The primary objective of INDUSTRAT is the acquisition of strategic industrial marketing skills. A competitive performance short of your expectations should not diminish your interest and enjoyment of this simulation. Past experience shows that lessons learned by confronting difficult situations are frequently of greater educational value than easy victories. The creators of INDUSTRAT would accordingly like to wish you a challenging experience.

glossary

Index of Rules and Constraints

Account size: small, medium, and large.

Adoption process: awareness, testing, supplementary, and major supplier.

Application: instrumentation, communication, and consumer products.

Base cost: estimated cost per unit at 100,000 units of experience.

Budget: maximum authorized expenditure managed by marketing.

DMU: decision making unit (see *Microsegmentation*).

Experience: cumulative production of products within the same technology.

Firms: five firms.

GNP: last three years (-2, -1, 0) 3 percent.

Geography: central, east, and west.

Growth: Korex sales grew 40 percent in year -6, but have slowed down.

Inflation: 10 percent at year 0 (15 percent in year -5).

Inventory: holding cost at LIFO value, charged to annual contribution.

Korex: product has been on the market for 15 years at year 0.

Licensing: when one firm's products uses another firm's development project (see *Royalties*).

List price change: maximum annual variation accepted is 30 percent.

Macrosegmentation: by geography, account size (potential), and application.

Market research: 16 studies available for sale annually (see Exhibit 4-1).

Microsegmentation: production, engineering, purchasing, and general managers.

Minimum base cost: lower limit for a given R&D department and given specifications.

Monetary unit: IM, $.

Obsolete inventory: When a successful development project (for change in product specifications or base costs) is actually used, the remaining inventory is automatically obsolete, and automatically charged to contribution at LIFO unless another arrangement is made with the INDUSTRAT administrator.

Period: each represents one year.

Physical characteristics: For Korex at Year 0, see Exhibit 2-1. For Lomex see Exhibit 2-2.

Population: 250 million.

Price discount: maximum authorized to the salesforce is 10 percent.

Production: automatic upward or downward adjustment of up to 20 percent of plan.

Products: each firm may sell up to 10 products and starts with four.

Project name: defines a single set of physical characteristics, which remain identical until completion. Only base costs may be changed. Any change in one of the four physical characteristics will be ignored.

Royalties: automatic 3 percent of sales at list price. Minimum annual royalty lump sum payment is negotiable (see *Licensing*).

Sales commission: Maximum authorized to award the salesforce is 20 percent.

Sales organization: May be organized along the geographic, size, or application segmentation schemes.

Technology: five for Korex (see Exhibit 5-1) and one for Lomex.

appendix A

Sample Company Report

The following represents the sample company report of Firm 3 in Period 5 of an IN-DUSTRAT simulation. This is only an example, and the data that it contains should not be used in making your decisions.

(In thousand $ except when indicated)

1. FINANCIAL RESULTS

```
****************************************************************
PRODUCT NAME        *  LIFE  *  KILT  *  KILL  *  KISS  *  KIDU  *
****************************************************************
PRODUCTION          * 80000 * 18470 *  3600 * 21599 * 32399 * UNITS
UNITS SOLD          * 47601 * 18470 *  8908 * 21599 * 42563 * UNITS
INVENTORY           * 32398 *     0 *     0 *     0 *     0 * UNITS
                    *       *       *       *       *       *
LIST PRICE          *   200 *   390 *   440 *   500 *   525 * $
AVERAGE PRICE       *   199 *   379 *   426 *   480 *   484 * $
                    *       *       *       *       *       *
MAX PRICE DISCOUNT  *    10 *     5 *     5 *     5 *    10 * %
UNIT MANUF COST     *    92 *   178 *   298 *   279 *   229 * $
UNIT LICENSING COST *     0 *     0 *     0 *     0 *     0 * $
UNIT COMMISSION     *    13 *    18 *    21 *    24 *    24 * $
TOTAL UNIT COST     *   106 *   197 *   319 *   303 *   253 * $
                    *       *       *       *       *       *
REVENUES FROM SALES *  9520 *  7016 *  3798 * 10381 * 20623 *
MANUFACTURING COSTS *  4391 *  3289 *  2655 *  6044 *  9759 *
LICENSING COSTS     *     0 *     0 *     0 *     0 *     0 *
SALES COMMISSIONS   *   666 *   350 *   189 *   519 *  1031 *
PROMOTION           *   600 *    75 *   100 *   200 *   200 *
PRODUCT ADVERTISING *   103 *     1 *    17 *    17 *    17 *
TECHNICAL SUPPORT   *   534 *   142 *   178 *   178 *   391 *
                    *       *       *       *       *       *
INVENTORY HOLD COSTS*   478 *     0 *     0 *     0 *     0 *
GROSS MKTG CONTRIB  *  2746 *  3156 *   657 *  3422 *  9223 *
****************************************************************
```

```
************
PRODUCT NAME        *  KINE  *
************
PRODUCTION          * 35120 * UNITS
UNITS SOLD          * 35120 * UNITS
INVENTORY           *     0 * UNITS
LIST PRICE          *   520 * $
AVERAGE PRICE       *   500 * $
MAX PRICE DISCOUNT  *     5 * %
UNIT MANUF COST     *   266 * $
UNIT LICENSING COST *     0 * $
UNIT COMMISSION     *    25 * $
TOTAL UNIT COST     *   291 * $
REVENUES FROM SALES * 17560 *
MANUFACTURING COSTS *  9367 *
LICENSING COSTS     *     0 *
SALES COMMISSIONS   *   878 *
PROMOTION           *   300 *
PRODUCT ADVERTISING *    17 *
TECHNICAL SUPPORT   *   356 *
INVENTORY HOLD COSTS*     0 *
GROSS MKTG CONTRIB  *  6640 *
************
```

GLOBAL RESULTS

```
TOTAL GROSS MKTG CONTRIBUTION...........     25847
FIXED SALES FORCE COSTS.................      4746
SALES FORCE TRAINING COSTS..............       200
CORPORATE COMMUNICATIONS................         0
RESEARCH................................         0
DEVELOPMENT.............................       655
MARKET RESEARCH.........................      1017

OPERATIONAL MKTG CONTRIBUTION...........     19229

REVENUES FROM LICENSES..................         0
EXCEPTIONAL COST OR PROFIT..............       211

NET MKTG CONTRIBUTION...................     19439

BUDGET FOR NEXT PERIOD..................      7981
```

2. MARKETING RESULTS

PRODUCT NAME	LIFE	KILT	KILL	KISS	KIDU
% TESTS PERFORMED	8.8	1.5	1.0	2.2	4.4
% CLIENTS SUPP SOURC	12.3	7.1	0.0	4.9	12.0
% CLIENTS PRIM SOURC	80.1	2.2	1.4	3.0	6.0
MS VOLUME SUPP SOURC	3.9	3.6	0.0	2.6	6.0
MS VOLUME PRIM SOURC	81.1	2.6	1.9	3.6	6.8
TOTAL MS VOLUME	65.4	2.9	1.4	3.3	6.6
MS VALUE SUPPL SOURC	0.9	2.4	0.0	2.3	5.2
MS VALUE PRIM SOURC	48.7	1.8	1.4	3.1	6.0
TOTAL MS VALUE	29.6	2.0	1.1	2.9	5.7

PRODUCT NAME	KINE
% TESTS PERFORMED	3.2
% CLIENTS SUPP SOURC	14.7
% CLIENTS PRIM SOURC	4.6
MS VOLUME SUPP SOURC	6.8
MS VOLUME PRIM SOURC	4.9
TOTAL MS VOLUME	5.4
MS VALUE SUPPL SOURC	6.1
MS VALUE PRIM SOURC	4.4
TOTAL MS VALUE	4.9

3. SALES AND TECHNICAL FORCES

```
NUMBER OF SALESPERSONS        :       79.
ORGANIZATIONAL STRUCTURE      :   END PRODUCT
SALES FORCE TRAINING ($)      :   200000.
```

ALLOCATION OF SALESFORCE   :

```
                  *************************
GEOGRAPHY         *  .30  *  .40  *  .30  *
SIZE              *  .34  *  .33  *  .33  *
END PRODUCT       *  .10  *  .40  *  .50  *
                  *************************
DMU               * .30 * .24 * .29 * .18 *
                  *************************
```

```
NUMBER OF TECHNICIANS         :       40.
TECHNICAL FORCE TRAINING      :   150000.
```

ALLOCATION OF TECHNICAL FORCE   :

```
                  *************************
GEOGRAPHY         *  .30  *  .40  *  .30  *
SIZE              *  .34  *  .33  *  .33  *
END PRODUCT       *  .10  *  .40  *  .50  *
                  *************************
DMU               * .45 * .45 * .05 * .05 *
                  *************************
```

4. MESSAGES

- MESSAGE NUMBER   1 :

Obsolete inventory of product "KISS",
charged at transfer cost.

- MESSAGE NUMBER   2 :

Obsolete inventory of product "KINE",
charged at transfer cost.

- MESSAGE NUMBER   3 :

Project name "PLIA ", has already been used.
Name of current project was changed to PLIAA.

- MESSAGE NUMBER   4 :

Allocated marketing budget for the
current period was exceeded by $ 935.
Expenditures were cut on   :
                                - Corporate marketing
                                - Product advertising

5. RESEARCH AND DEVELOPMENT

RESEARCH

TECHNOLOGY	1	2	3	4	5
CUMULATIVE INVEST	0	5500	8000	0	13050
YEARS ABOVE MIN INV	0	2	2	0	3
STATUS	NO	OK	OK	NO	OK
MIN TOTAL INVEST	3351	5585	5585	8936	11170
PROP TOTAL INVEST	6702	11170	11170	13404	16755
MIN ANNUAL INVEST	1117	1675	1675	2234	2234

DEVELOPMENT

NAME	PKILT	PKISS	PKIDU	PKINE	PKIST
TECHNOLOGY	3	2	2	3	2
CUM EXPENDITURES	300	400	500	300	270
STATUS	OK	OK	OK	OK	OK
CHARACTERISTIC 1	2800	3000	6000	2800	3000
CHARACTERISTIC 2	100	40	55	80	40
CHARACTERISTIC 3	90	100	120	110	100
CHARACTERISTIC 4	600	550	750	700	550
BASE COST	211	401	337	316	284 $

NAME	PKIDS	PKIND	PKILL	PLIA	PKISU
TECHNOLOGY	2	3	3	5	2
CUM EXPENDITURES	270	300	270	13050	250
STATUS	OK	OK	OK	OK	OK
CHARACTERISTIC 1	6000	2800	2800	17	5000
CHARACTERISTIC 2	55	80	60	101	40
CHARACTERISTIC 3	120	110	90	43	100
CHARACTERISTIC 4	750	700	600	224	550
BASE COST	267	285	284	100	285 $

```
                              **********************
NAME                          *  PLICK  *  PLIAA  *
                              **********************
TECHNOLOGY                    *      5  *      5  *
CUM EXPENDITURES              *    660  *      5  *
STATUS                        *     OK  *     NO  *
                              **********************
CHARACTERISTIC 1              *     20  *     17  *
CHARACTERISTIC 2              *    100  *    101  *
CHARACTERISTIC 3              *     50  *     43  *
CHARACTERISTIC 4              *    500  *    224  *
BASE COST                     *     76  *     50  *
                              **********************
```

BASE COST FOR PROJECT PLIAA TOO LOW. MINIMUM GUARANTEED FEASIBLE BASE
COST IS 61 $. ADDITIONAL BUDGET REQUIRED : 554 THOUSAND $. IF YOU
PURSUE THIS PROJECT, REMEMBER TO INCREASE BOTH BASE COST AND REQUIRED
BUDGET BY INFLATION.

6. CUMULATIVE RESULTS

```
*********************************************************
PRODUCT NAME      *  KILT  *  KISS  *  KIDU  *  KINE  *  KILL  *
*********************************************************
INTRODUCTION PERIOD *    -4 *    -2 *    -4 *    -5 *     4 *
LAST MODIF PERIOD   *    -4 *     5 *     4 *     5 *     4 *
                    *       *       *       *       *       *
UNITS SOLD          * 100315 * 153155 * 246524 * 249568 * 11600 * UNITS
REVENUES FROM SALES *  31653 *  73546 * 110758 * 108022 *  4999 *
MANUFACTURING COSTS *  14571 *  37439 *  49715 *  49367 *  3385 *
LICENSING COSTS     *      0 *      0 *      0 *      0 *     0 *
SALES COMMISSIONS   *   1351 *   4718 *   5193 *   6671 *   249 *
PROMOTION           *    625 *   1500 *   1360 *   1950 *   200 *
PRODUCT ADVERTISING *     61 *    157 *    457 *    407 *   117 *
TECHNICAL SUPPORT   *    577 *   1067 *   1258 *   1546 *   309 *
                    *       *       *       *       *       *
GROSS MKTG CONTRIB  *  14379 *  28437 *  52027 *  47911 *   478 *
*********************************************************
```

```
**********
PRODUCT NAME      *  LIFE  *
**********
INTRODUCTION PERIOD *     5 *
LAST MODIF PERIOD   *     5 *
                    *       *
UNITS SOLD          * 47601 *
REVENUES FROM SALES *  9520 *
MANUFACTURING COSTS *  4391 *
LICENSING COSTS     *     0 *
SALES COMMISSIONS   *   666 *
PROMOTION           *   600 *
PRODUCT ADVERTISING *   103 *
TECHNICAL SUPPORT   *   534 *
                    *       *
GROSS MKTG CONTRIB  *  2746 *
**********
```

```
TOTAL GROSS MKTG CONTRIBUTION...........    145981
FIXED SALES FORCE COSTS.................     15816
SALES FORCE TRAINING COSTS..............       400
CORPORATE COMMUNICATIONS................        95
RESEARCH................................     13050
DEVELOPMENT.............................      2025
MARKET RESEARCH.........................      1899

OPERATIONAL MKTG CONTRIBUTION...........    112695

REVENUES FROM LICENSES..................         0
EXCEPTIONAL COST OR PROFIT..............      1700

NET MKTG CONTRIBUTION...................    114396
```

7. NEWSLETTER

Environmental Factors

    - GNP GROWTH RATE THIS PERIOD   =   2.5 %
    - ESTIMATED GNP GROWTH RATE NEXT PERIOD   =   1.5 %
    - INFLATION RATE   =   13.0 %
    - ESTIMATED INFLATION RATE NEXT PERIOD   =   10.0 %

Cost Factors

    - FIXED ANNUAL COST OF SALESPERSON NEXT PERIOD   =   66772 $
    - COST OF HIRING A SALESPERSON NEXT PERIOD   =   11128 $
    - COST OF FIRING A SALESPERSON NEXT PERIOD   =   33386 $
    - FIXED ANNUAL COST OF A TECHNICIAN NEXT PERIOD =   44555 $
    - COST OF HIRING A TECHNICIAN NEXT PERIOD   =   7425 $
    - COST OF FIRING A TECHNICIAN NEXT PERIOD   =   22277 $

    - COST OF MARKETING RESEARCH STUDIES (IN $) =

1 :	18336.	2 :	101866.	3 :	20373.	4 :	30560.	5 :	40746.
6 :	24448.	7 :	81492.	8 :	122239.	9 :	16298.	10 :	20373.
11 :	30560.	12 :	40746.	13 :	24448.	14 :	81492.	15 :	16298.
16 :	91679.								

    - INVENTORY HOLDING COST (%) =   16.0

Messages from corporate lawyers

    - THE GOVERNMENT HAS DECIDED TO CONTROL PRICES. PRICES OF EXISTING
      PRODUCTS CANNOT BE INCREASED BY MORE THAN 5.0 %.

Newsflash

LOMEX TECHNOLOGY NOW AVAILABLE FROM COMPANY 3. FOR INFORMATION CONTACT
CORPORATE MANAGEMENT (I.E. THE ADMINISTRATOR)

Product Specifications

```
*******************************************************************
* PRODUCT * LAST * TEC * PROJECT *    CHARACTERISTICS    * BASE  *
* NAME    * MODIF*     *         *  1 *  2 *  3  *   4   * COST  *
*******************************************************************
*   KALA  * -3.  * 2.  * PKALA  *10000*  50* 100*  750*  316 *
*   KAST  * -2.  * 1.  * PKAST  * 1500*  20*  90*  600*  633 *
*   KAMI  * -5.  * 2.  * PKAMI  * 6500*  40* 110*  700*  369 *
*   KAPE  * -4.  * 1.  * PKAPE  * 1500*  45*  85*  650*  591 *
*   KAMO  *  3.  * 2.  * PKAMO  * 4000*  55* 110*  700*  368 *
*   KAMU  *  4.  * 2.  * PKAMU  * 5500*  58* 110*  700*  367 *
*   KAPI  *  4.  * 1.  * PKAPI  * 4000*  50*  85*  650*  440 *
*   KENT  *  5.  * 3.  * PKEXW  * 4000*  60*  90*  700*  324 *
*   KEPI  *  3.  * 1.  * PKEZZ  * 4000*  50*  95*  600*  366 *
*   KEEP  *  4.  * 3.  * PKEXY  * 3000*  45* 130*  700*  367 *
*   KELY  * -3.  * 3.  * PKELY  * 1300*  50* 120*  650*  485 *
*   KENE  *  5.  * 3.  * PKEXE  * 3000*  75* 110*  700*  259 *
*   KETE  *  3.  * 3.  * PKEWW  * 4000*  90* 100*  700*  407 *
*   LIFE  *  5.  * 5.  * PLIA   *   17* 101*  43*  224*  100 *
*   KILT  * -4.  * 3.  * PKILT  * 2800* 100*  90*  600*  211 *
*   KILL  *  4.  * 3.  * PKILL  * 2800*  60*  90*  600*  284 *
*   KISS  *  5.  * 2.  * PKISU  * 5000*  40* 100*  550*  285 *
*   KIDU  *  4.  * 2.  * PKIDS  * 6000*  55* 120*  750*  267 *
*   KINE  *  5.  * 3.  * PKIND  * 2800*  80* 110*  700*  285 *
*   KOPA  * -2.  * 1.  * PKOPA  * 3500*  20* 115*  550*  467 *
*   KOLD  *  4.  * 2.  * PKOID  * 6000*  55* 120*  750*  274 *
*   KOPS  *  4.  * 2.  * PKOID  * 6000*  55* 120*  750*  274 *
*   KOOK  *  3.  * 2.  * PKOPS  * 3000*  45* 120*  600*  523 *
*   KOLI  *  4.  * 2.  * PKOLI  * 3000*  60* 130*  650*  285 *
*   KUTE  *  5.  * 4.  * PKUA   * 6172*  77*  88*  630*  198 *
*   LUVV  *  5.  * 5.  * PLUA   *    8* 127*  27*  319*   91 *
*******************************************************************
```

INFORMATION ON MARKET "K"

```
************************************************************************
* PRODUCT * VOLUME  * VOLUME *ACTUAL  *  VALUE   * VALUE  *
* NAME    * SALES   * MARKET *SELLING*  SALES    * MARKET *
*         *         * SHARE  *PRICE   *  (000 $) * SHARE  *
************************************************************************
*  KALA   *  19165  *  3.0   *  585  *  11211   *  3.1   *
*  KAST   *   8978  *  1.4   *  671  *   6028   *  1.7   *
*  KAMI   *  37586  *  5.8   *  513  *  19319   *  5.4   *
*  KAPE   *  16994  *  2.6   *  623  *  10599   *  2.9   *
*  KAMO   *  27992  *  4.3   *  551  *  15443   *  4.3   *
*  KAMU   *  10893  *  1.7   *  532  *   5806   *  1.6   *
*  KAPI   *   3711  *  0.6   *  570  *   2115   *  0.6   *
*  KENT   *  20391  *  3.1   *  907  *  18499   *  5.1   *
*  KEPI   *  25251  *  3.9   *  696  *  17575   *  4.9   *
*  KEEP   *  23252  *  3.6   *  672  *  15625   *  4.3   *
*  KELY   *  27324  *  4.2   *  511  *  13979   *  3.9   *
*  KENE   *  39702  *  6.1   *  510  *  20285   *  5.6   *
*  KETE   *  24000  *  3.7   *  552  *  13265   *  3.7   *
*  KILT   *  18470  *  2.9   *  379  *   7016   *  2.0   *
*  KILL   *   8908  *  1.4   *  426  *   3798   *  1.1   *
*  KISS   *  21600  *  3.3   *  480  *  10381   *  2.9   *
*  KIDU   *  42563  *  6.6   *  484  *  20623   *  5.7   *
*  KINE   *  35120  *  5.4   *  500  *  17560   *  4.9   *
*  KOPA   *  17436  *  2.7   *  697  *  12158   *  3.4   *
*  KOLD   *  71738  * 11.1   *  495  *  35563   *  9.9   *
*  KOPS   *  63097  *  9.7   *  560  *  35376   *  9.8   *
*  KOOK   *  19265  *  3.0   *  676  *  13038   *  3.6   *
*  KOLI   *   4412  *  0.7   *  533  *   2355   *  0.7   *
*  KUTE   *  60000  *  9.3   *  528  *  31726   *  8.8   *
*         *         *        *       *          *        *
* TOTAL   * 647860  * 100.0  *       * 359354   * 100.0  *
************************************************************************
```

AVERAGE ACTUAL SELLING PRICE :   554 $

TOTAL NUMBER OF CLIENTS   :   17304

INFORMATION ON MARKET "L"

```
**************************************************************
* PRODUCT *  VOLUME  * VOLUME *ACTUAL * VALUE  *  VALUE   *
* NAME    *  SALES   * MARKET *SELLING* SALES  *  MARKET  *
*         *          * SHARE  *PRICE  * (000 $)*  SHARE   *
**************************************************************
*  LIFE   *  47601   *  65.4  *  199  *  9520  *   29.6   *
*  LUVV   *  25218   *  34.6  *  900  * 22696  *   70.4   *
*         *          *        *       *        *          *
*  TOTAL  *  72820   * 100.0  *       * 32217  *  100.0   *
**************************************************************
```

AVERAGE ACTUAL SELLING PRICE   :   442 $

TOTAL NUMBER OF CLIENTS   :   10778

appendix B

Sample Marketing Research Studies

The following contains the marketing research studies requested by Firm 3 in Period 5 of the INDUSTRAT simulation, as indicated in the sample decision form in Exhibit 6-1. This is only an example; the data that it contains should not be used in making your decisions.

MARKET RESEARCH　　　FIRM 3　　　PERIOD 5　　　INDUSTRY A

STUDY 1　:　SUPPLIER SURVEY
****

Telephone survey of 30 companies. First number indicates
percentage having a satisfactory knowledge of suppliers.
Second number indicates relative preference for each supplier.

	AGGREGATE				EAST				CENTRAL				WEST			
	PRO	ENG	PUR	GAL	PRO	ENG	PUR	GAL	PRO	ENG	PUR	GAL	PRO	ENG	PUR	GAL
FIRM 1																
AWA	80.	80.	80.	44.	83.	82.	81.	43.	81.	83.	83.	42.	81.	82.	80.	45.
PRE	13.	13.	11.	7.	8.	9.	9.	4.	8.	11.	9.	6.	18.	17.	13.	10.
FIRM 2																
AWA	77.	77.	77.	43.	77.	78.	76.	44.	76.	76.	76.	41.	77.	77.	75.	45.
PRE	17.	25.	14.	11.	19.	27.	12.	7.	15.	20.	10.	7.	19.	27.	18.	15.
FIRM 3																
AWA	64.	64.	63.	49.	64.	67.	62.	50.	62.	65.	62.	51.	61.	65.	62.	49.
PRE	23.	16.	23.	27.	26.	16.	26.	28.	21.	17.	21.	28.	23.	15.	22.	25.
FIRM 4																
AWA	82.	83.	81.	52.	80.	81.	82.	54.	80.	83.	81.	56.	80.	81.	81.	50.
PRE	28.	29.	30.	31.	37.	33.	36.	44.	36.	33.	40.	42.	18.	24.	22.	18.
FIRM 5																
AWA	69.	70.	71.	57.	70.	70.	71.	58.	69.	71.	71.	56.	70.	70.	69.	58.
PRE	19.	17.	22.	24.	12.	14.	18.	17.	21.	19.	19.	18.	22.	16.	24.	31.

GEOGRAPHICAL SEGMENTATION

STUDY 2 :   SURVEY ON PERCEPTIONS OF SUPPLIERS
****

Telephone survey of 30 companies. Three dimensions
were found to be of determinant importance
in explaining the perceptions of suppliers :

        Dimension 1 : Technical aspects (TEC)
        Dimension 2 : Commercial aspects (COM)
        Dimension 3 : General reputation as a corporation (REP)

    * RELATIVE IMPORTANCE OF DIMENSIONS
    =====================================

Relative weight for each dimension.
(Sum over the three dimensions is equal to 100.)

	AGGREGATE				EAST				GEOGRAPHICAL SEGMENTATION CENTRAL				WEST			
	PRO	ENG	PUR	GAL	PRO	ENG	PUR	GAL	PRO	ENG	PUR	GAL	PRO	ENG	PUR	GAL
TEC	28.	45.	25.	20.	28.	45.	25.	20.	28.	45.	25.	20.	28.	45.	25.	20.
COM	55.	31.	54.	46.	55.	31.	54.	46.	55.	31.	54.	46.	55.	30.	54.	46.
REP	17.	24.	21.	34.	16.	24.	21.	34.	17.	24.	21.	34.	17.	24.	21.	34.

    * IDEAL POINTS
    ==============

Most desired combination on 1-7 scales.
(1 = low, 7 = high)

	AGGREGATE				EAST				GEOGRAPHICAL SEGMENTATION CENTRAL				WEST			
	PRO	ENG	PUR	GAL	PRO	ENG	PUR	GAL	PRO	ENG	PUR	GAL	PRO	ENG	PUR	GAL
TEC	4.9	4.4	3.9	3.7	4.8	4.4	3.8	3.6	4.8	4.3	3.8	3.6	4.8	4.3	3.9	3.6
COM	3.5	3.3	5.3	4.8	3.6	3.3	5.2	4.8	3.6	3.3	5.3	4.8	3.6	3.3	5.2	4.8
REP	4.7	5.1	4.1	4.9	4.7	5.2	4.0	4.9	4.7	5.1	4.1	5.0	4.7	5.1	4.0	4.9

* PERCEPTIONS OF SUPPLIERS
============================

Perceptions on 1-7 scales.
(1 = low, 7 = high)

. TECHNICAL ASPECTS

	GEOGRAPHICAL SEGMENTATION			
FIRM	AGGREGATE	EAST	CENTRAL	WEST
	PRO ENG PUR GAL	PRO ENG PUR GAL	PRO ENG PUR GAL	PRO ENG PUR GAL
1	3.0 2.8 1.5 1.3	2.3 2.4 1.4 1.2	2.5 2.4 1.4 1.2	3.8 3.3 1.6 1.4
2	3.7 3.3 2.0 1.6	3.7 3.5 2.0 1.6	3.6 3.1 1.9 1.4	3.8 3.4 2.2 1.7
3	3.6 3.3 2.3 2.4	3.5 3.4 2.4 2.5	3.6 3.2 2.2 2.3	3.6 3.2 2.4 2.4
4	4.0 3.4 2.9 2.2	4.0 3.5 2.8 2.4	4.1 3.4 3.0 2.3	3.8 3.4 2.7 2.1
5	4.1 3.6 3.2 3.4	3.6 3.5 3.3 3.4	4.3 3.7 3.3 3.3	4.3 3.7 3.4 3.4

. COMMERCIAL ASPECTS

	GEOGRAPHICAL SEGMENTATION			
FIRM	AGGREGATE	EAST	CENTRAL	WEST
	PRO ENG PUR GAL	PRO ENG PUR GAL	PRO ENG PUR GAL	PRO ENG PUR GAL
1	2.8 2.5 1.2 1.0	2.1 2.1 1.2 1.0	2.3 2.1 1.1 1.0	3.6 3.1 1.3 1.0
2	3.4 3.1 2.1 1.4	3.4 3.2 2.1 1.5	3.1 2.7 1.5 1.0	3.6 3.3 2.6 1.8
3	3.0 2.9 2.9 2.8	3.1 3.0 3.0 2.9	2.8 2.5 3.0 2.7	3.0 3.0 2.9 2.8
4	3.2 2.9 3.0 2.5	3.1 2.9 3.3 2.9	3.2 3.0 3.5 2.9	3.4 2.9 2.5 2.0
5	3.4 3.1 3.4 3.5	3.0 3.0 3.3 3.6	3.6 3.2 3.5 3.3	3.5 3.0 3.4 3.7

. GENERAL REPUTATION

	GEOGRAPHICAL SEGMENTATION			
FIRM	AGGREGATE	EAST	CENTRAL	WEST
	PRO ENG PUR GAL	PRO ENG PUR GAL	PRO ENG PUR GAL	PRO ENG PUR GAL
1	2.8 2.5 2.7 1.5	2.1 2.1 1.4 1.0	2.2 2.0 1.2 1.0	3.6 3.1 4.3 2.3
2	4.4 4.6 4.3 4.4	4.4 4.5 4.4 4.6	4.5 4.5 4.2 4.4	4.4 4.6 4.2 4.5
3	3.3 3.2 2.6 3.0	3.2 3.3 2.6 3.1	3.3 3.1 2.6 3.0	3.4 3.2 2.5 2.9
4	4.4 4.3 3.9 3.9	4.5 4.7 4.2 4.9	4.5 4.0 4.5 4.2	3.9 4.0 3.3 3.2
5	3.7 3.3 3.1 3.0	3.3 3.2 3.1 3.0	4.0 3.5 3.0 2.8	3.7 3.2 3.1 3.1

STUDY 3 : PRODUCT AWARENESS AND PREFERENCE SURVEY - KOREX MARKET
****

Telephone survey of 50 companies.

* PRODUCT AWARENESS
====================

Percentage having a satisfactory knowledge of product.

					GEOGRAPHICAL				SEGMENTATION						
PRODUCT	AGGREGATE				EAST				CENTRAL				WEST			
	PRO	ENG	PUR	GAL	PRO	ENG	PUR	GAL	PRO	ENG	PUR	GAL	PRO	ENG	PUR	GAL
KALA	34.	53.	34.	22.	30.	48.	29.	18.	31.	49.	31.	20.	38.	57.	38.	26.
KAST	26.	46.	25.	16.	22.	41.	21.	13.	24.	42.	22.	14.	30.	50.	29.	19.
KAMI	53.	70.	51.	38.	48.	66.	46.	33.	49.	67.	48.	35.	57.	73.	56.	43.
KAPE	38.	60.	37.	24.	34.	56.	32.	20.	35.	57.	33.	22.	42.	64.	41.	28.
KAMO	41.	46.	38.	31.	35.	39.	32.	26.	38.	42.	34.	28.	46.	51.	43.	36.
KAMU	27.	31.	26.	23.	23.	27.	22.	19.	24.	28.	23.	20.	32.	36.	30.	26.
KAPI	20.	24.	17.	16.	17.	20.	14.	13.	18.	21.	15.	14.	23.	27.	20.	18.
KENT	54.	65.	54.	38.	55.	66.	54.	38.	52.	64.	52.	35.	55.	66.	55.	39.
KEPI	48.	60.	47.	32.	49.	61.	48.	32.	47.	58.	45.	30.	49.	60.	48.	33.
KEEP	52.	67.	51.	33.	53.	68.	52.	34.	51.	66.	50.	31.	53.	68.	52.	34.
KELY	50.	63.	49.	32.	50.	64.	49.	33.	48.	62.	47.	30.	50.	63.	50.	33.
KENE	55.	60.	55.	43.	56.	62.	56.	43.	52.	58.	53.	40.	56.	61.	57.	44.
KETE	48.	54.	48.	37.	50.	55.	49.	37.	45.	51.	45.	34.	49.	55.	49.	38.
KILT	28.	38.	25.	14.	30.	41.	27.	15.	27.	37.	24.	13.	27.	38.	25.	14.
KILL	15.	14.	15.	12.	16.	15.	15.	12.	15.	14.	14.	12.	15.	14.	15.	12.
KISS	40.	49.	37.	23.	43.	52.	39.	24.	39.	47.	36.	22.	40.	49.	37.	23.
KIDU	44.	51.	42.	28.	46.	54.	43.	29.	43.	50.	40.	27.	44.	51.	42.	28.
KINE	49.	61.	48.	31.	51.	63.	49.	32.	48.	60.	46.	30.	49.	61.	48.	31.
KOPA	41.	58.	43.	28.	44.	61.	45.	30.	46.	63.	47.	32.	37.	54.	38.	25.
KOLD	65.	76.	66.	52.	68.	78.	69.	55.	70.	79.	71.	56.	60.	72.	62.	48.
KOPS	64.	74.	65.	51.	68.	77.	68.	54.	69.	78.	70.	55.	59.	70.	61.	47.
KOOK	45.	64.	46.	30.	47.	66.	48.	32.	49.	67.	50.	33.	41.	61.	43.	27.
KOLI	25.	26.	25.	21.	27.	29.	28.	23.	30.	31.	30.	25.	20.	21.	20.	17.
KUTE	44.	58.	46.	38.	39.	54.	43.	37.	43.	56.	42.	36.	48.	61.	49.	40.

* PRODUCT PREFERENCE
=====================

Percentage of individuals stating a greater
preference for a given product, weighted by the
purchase volume of the corresponding client companies.

PRODUCT	AGGRGATE				EAST				GEOGRAPHICAL SEGMENTATION CENTRAL				WEST			
	PRO	ENG	PUR	GAL	PRO	ENG	PUR	GAL	PRO	ENG	PUR	GAL	PRO	ENG	PUR	GAL
KALA	3.	3.	2.	2.	2.	3.	2.	2.	3.	3.	2.	2.	3.	4.	3.	3.
KAST	1.	1.	1.	1.	1.	1.	1.	1.	1.	1.	1.	1.	1.	2.	1.	1.
KAMI	5.	5.	5.	7.	5.	5.	5.	6.	5.	5.	5.	7.	6.	6.	6.	9.
KAPE	2.	3.	2.	2.	2.	2.	2.	2.	2.	3.	2.	2.	3.	3.	2.	2.
KAMO	4.	4.	4.	4.	4.	3.	3.	3.	4.	4.	3.	4.	5.	5.	4.	5.
KAMU	3.	3.	4.	4.	3.	3.	3.	4.	3.	3.	4.	4.	4.	4.	5.	5.
KAPI	1.	1.	1.	1.	1.	1.	1.	1.	1.	1.	1.	1.	2.	2.	2.	2.
KENT	3.	3.	2.	2.	3.	3.	2.	2.	3.	3.	2.	2.	3.	3.	2.	2.
KEPI	4.	4.	3.	3.	4.	4.	3.	3.	3.	4.	3.	2.	4.	4.	3.	3.
KEEP	3.	3.	3.	2.	3.	3.	3.	3.	3.	3.	3.	2.	3.	3.	3.	2.
KELY	4.	3.	4.	3.	4.	3.	4.	4.	4.	3.	4.	3.	4.	3.	4.	3.
KENE	6.	5.	6.	5.	6.	5.	6.	6.	5.	5.	5.	5.	6.	5.	6.	6.
KETE	6.	6.	5.	5.	7.	7.	5.	5.	6.	6.	4.	4.	6.	6.	5.	5.
KILT	3.	2.	3.	2.	3.	2.	3.	2.	3.	2.	2.	2.	3.	2.	2.	2.
KILL	2.	1.	2.	2.	2.	1.	2.	2.	2.	1.	2.	2.	2.	1.	2.	2.
KISS	3.	3.	4.	3.	4.	3.	4.	3.	3.	3.	4.	3.	3.	3.	4.	3.
KIDU	6.	6.	8.	7.	7.	6.	8.	8.	6.	5.	7.	7.	6.	5.	8.	7.
KINE	5.	4.	5.	4.	5.	4.	5.	4.	5.	4.	5.	4.	5.	4.	5.	4.
KOPA	3.	3.	2.	2.	3.	3.	2.	2.	3.	3.	3.	2.	2.	2.	2.	2.
KOLD	9.	8.	13.	12.	9.	8.	14.	13.	10.	8.	14.	13.	8.	7.	11.	10.
KOPS	9.	8.	10.	10.	9.	8.	11.	10.	9.	8.	11.	11.	7.	7.	9.	8.
KOOK	3.	3.	3.	2.	3.	3.	3.	2.	3.	3.	3.	2.	2.	3.	2.	2.
KOLI	3.	2.	3.	3.	3.	2.	3.	3.	3.	2.	3.	3.	2.	1.	2.	2.
KUTE	9.	15.	6.	11.	8.	14.	6.	11.	9.	15.	6.	11.	10.	16.	7.	11.

STUDY 4 : DEMAND ANALYSIS - KOREX MARKET
****

Estimates based on statistical sources, interviews
in 30 companies and managerial judgment.

| | | GEOGRAPHICAL | SEGMENTATION | |
	AGGREGATE	EAST	CENTRAL	WEST
NUMBER OF CLIENTS	17305.	3939.	5264.	8102.
TOTAL VALUE (000 $)	359354.	103049.	177025.	79281.
TOTAL VOLUME (000 UNITS)	648.	186.	319.	143.
AVERAGE/CLIENT (VALUE 000 $)	20766.	26162.	33631.	9785.
AVERAGE/CLIENT (VOLUME 000 UNITS)	37.	47.	61.	18.
PRIMARY SOURCING (% VALUE)	73.	74.	72.	74.
PRIMARY SOURCING (% VOLUME)	73.	75.	72.	74.
AVERAGE NUMBER OF SUPPLIERS PER CLIENT	2.59	2.66	2.64	2.38

STUDY 5 : MARKET SHARES SURVEY - KOREX MARKET
****

Estimates based on survey of 40 companies.

* AGGREGATE MARKET SHARES
===========================

	% TESTS	% CLIENTS		% VOLUME			% VALUE		
PRODUCTS		SUPPL	PRIM	SUPPL	PRIM	TOTAL	SUPPL	PRIM	TOTAL
KALA	2.2	8.6	3.0	3.4	2.8	3.0	3.6	3.0	3.1
KAST	1.0	4.3	1.4	1.7	1.3	1.4	2.0	1.6	1.7
KAMI	4.5	13.9	6.2	5.7	5.9	5.8	5.2	5.4	5.4
KAPE	1.8	8.0	2.6	3.2	2.4	2.6	3.6	2.7	2.9
KAMO	3.3	14.5	4.6	5.2	4.0	4.3	5.1	4.0	4.3
KAMU	2.9	0.0	2.8	0.0	2.3	1.7	0.0	2.2	1.6
KAPI	1.2	0.0	0.9	0.0	0.8	0.6	0.0	0.8	0.6
KENT	2.2	9.2	3.0	3.9	2.9	3.1	6.3	4.7	5.1
KEPI	2.8	11.3	3.7	4.8	3.6	3.9	6.0	4.5	4.9
KEEP	2.3	10.0	3.2	4.5	3.3	3.6	5.3	4.0	4.3
KELY	2.6	10.9	3.5	5.3	3.8	4.2	4.8	3.5	3.9
KENE	3.8	17.0	5.4	7.7	5.6	6.1	7.0	5.2	5.6
KETE	4.6	0.0	5.4	0.0	5.0	3.7	0.0	5.0	3.7
KILT	1.5	7.1	2.2	3.6	2.6	2.9	2.4	1.8	2.0
KILL	1.0	0.0	1.4	0.0	1.9	1.4	0.0	1.4	1.1
KISS	2.2	4.9	3.0	2.6	3.6	3.3	2.3	3.1	2.9
KIDU	4.4	12.0	6.0	6.0	6.8	6.6	5.2	6.0	5.7
KINE	3.2	14.7	4.6	6.8	4.9	5.4	6.1	4.4	4.9
KOPA	2.1	6.2	2.7	2.7	2.7	2.7	3.4	3.4	3.4
KOLD	6.8	29.8	9.6	13.8	10.1	11.1	12.2	9.1	9.9
KOPS	6.6	27.3	8.9	12.0	8.9	9.7	12.0	9.1	9.8
KOOK	2.1	6.7	3.0	3.0	3.0	3.0	3.6	3.6	3.6
KOLI	1.8	0.0	0.8	0.0	0.9	0.7	0.0	0.9	0.7
KUTE	8.8	11.3	12.4	4.3	11.1	9.3	4.1	10.6	8.8

* MARKET SHARES AS PRIMARY SUPPLIER
=====================================

GEOGRAPHICAL SEGMENTATION

PRODUCTS	EAST % VOL	EAST % VAL	CENTRAL % VOL	CENTRAL % VAL	WEST % VOL	WEST % VAL
KALA	2.5	2.6	2.7	2.9	3.4	3.6
KAST	1.1	1.4	1.2	1.5	1.5	1.9
KAMI	5.3	5.0	5.7	5.3	6.9	6.4
KAPE	2.2	2.5	2.4	2.7	2.8	3.2
KAMO	3.5	3.5	3.9	3.9	4.9	4.9
KAMU	2.0	1.9	2.2	2.1	2.9	2.8
KAPI	0.7	0.7	0.7	0.8	1.0	1.0
KENT	3.0	4.9	2.8	4.6	2.9	4.7
KEPI	3.7	4.7	3.5	4.4	3.6	4.5
KEEP	3.4	4.1	3.2	3.9	3.3	4.0
KELY	4.0	3.7	3.7	3.5	3.8	3.5
KENE	5.8	5.4	5.4	5.0	5.7	5.3
KETE	5.5	5.5	4.7	4.7	5.1	5.1
KILT	2.8	2.0	2.5	1.7	2.4	1.7
KILL	1.9	1.5	1.9	1.4	1.8	1.4
KISS	3.7	3.3	3.5	3.1	3.5	3.1
KIDU	7.0	6.2	6.7	5.9	6.7	5.8
KINE	5.0	4.5	4.9	4.4	4.8	4.3
KOPA	2.7	3.5	2.9	3.7	2.0	2.5
KOLD	10.3	9.2	10.7	9.6	8.6	7.7
KOPS	9.1	9.2	9.5	9.6	7.6	7.7
KOOK	3.0	3.7	3.2	3.9	2.5	3.1
KOLI	0.9	0.9	1.1	1.0	0.6	0.6
KUTE	10.6	10.1	11.1	10.6	11.7	11.2

* MARKET SHARES AS SUPPLEMENTARY SUPPLIER
==

GEOGRAPHICAL SEGMENTATION

PRODUCTS	EAST % VOL	EAST % VAL	CENTRAL % VOL	CENTRAL % VAL	WEST % VOL	WEST % VAL
KALA	3.0	3.2	3.3	3.4	4.2	4.4
KAST	1.5	1.8	1.6	1.9	2.1	2.5
KAMI	5.1	4.7	5.5	5.0	6.8	6.2
KAPE	2.9	3.3	3.1	3.5	3.8	4.2
KAMO	4.5	4.4	5.0	4.9	6.6	6.5
KAMU	0.0	0.0	0.0	0.0	0.0	0.0
KAPI	0.0	0.0	0.0	0.0	0.0	0.0
KENT	4.0	6.4	3.8	6.2	3.9	6.3
KEPI	5.0	6.2	4.7	5.8	4.9	6.0
KEEP	4.6	5.5	4.4	5.2	4.5	5.4
KELY	5.6	5.1	5.2	4.7	5.3	4.9
KENE	8.0	7.3	7.4	6.7	8.0	7.3
KETE	0.0	0.0	0.0	0.0	0.0	0.0
KILT	4.0	2.7	3.4	2.3	3.5	2.4
KILL	0.0	0.0	0.0	0.0	0.0	0.0
KISS	2.8	2.4	2.6	2.2	2.6	2.2
KIDU	6.2	5.4	5.8	5.0	6.0	5.2
KINE	7.0	6.2	6.7	6.0	6.9	6.1
KOPA	2.8	3.4	3.0	3.7	2.0	2.5
KOLD	13.9	12.3	14.5	12.8	11.7	10.3
KOPS	12.1	12.1	12.7	12.7	10.1	10.1
KOOK	3.0	3.6	3.1	3.8	2.5	3.0
KOLI	0.0	0.0	0.0	0.0	0.0	0.0
KUTE	4.1	3.9	4.3	4.0	4.6	4.4

* MARKET SHARES TOTALS
=======================

GEOGRAPHICAL SEGMENTATION

	EAST		CENTRAL		WEST	
PRODUCTS	% VOL	% VAL	% VOL	% VAL	% VOL	% VAL
KALA	2.6	2.8	2.9	3.0	3.6	3.8
KAST	1.2	1.5	1.3	1.6	1.7	2.0
KAMI	5.3	4.9	5.6	5.2	6.8	6.3
KAPE	2.4	2.7	2.6	2.9	3.1	3.4
KAMO	3.8	3.7	4.2	4.2	5.3	5.3
KAMU	1.5	1.4	1.6	1.5	2.1	2.0
KAPI	0.5	0.5	0.5	0.6	0.7	0.8
KENT	3.2	5.3	3.1	5.1	3.1	5.1
KEPI	4.0	5.1	3.8	4.8	3.9	4.9
KEEP	3.7	4.4	3.5	4.3	3.6	4.4
KELY	4.4	4.0	4.1	3.8	4.2	3.9
KENE	6.3	5.9	5.9	5.5	6.3	5.8
KETE	4.1	4.1	3.4	3.4	3.8	3.8
KILT	3.1	2.2	2.7	1.9	2.7	1.9
KILL	1.4	1.1	1.3	1.0	1.4	1.0
KISS	3.5	3.0	3.3	2.8	3.3	2.8
KIDU	6.8	6.0	6.4	5.6	6.5	5.7
KINE	5.5	5.0	5.4	4.9	5.3	4.8
KOPA	2.7	3.5	3.0	3.7	2.0	2.5
KOLD	11.2	10.0	11.8	10.5	9.4	8.4
KOPS	9.9	10.0	10.4	10.5	8.2	8.3
KOOK	3.0	3.7	3.2	3.8	2.5	3.1
KOLI	0.7	0.7	0.8	0.7	0.5	0.4
KUTE	8.9	8.5	9.2	8.7	9.9	9.4

* PROPORTION OF PRODUCTS IN TESTS
======================================

GEOGRAPHICAL SEGMENTATION

PRODUCTS	EAST	CENTRAL	WEST
KALA	1.9	1.8	2.6
KAST	0.8	0.9	1.1
KAMI	4.0	3.7	5.3
KAPE	1.5	1.5	2.1
KAMO	2.7	2.8	4.0
KAMU	2.4	2.4	3.5
KAPI	1.0	1.0	1.5
KENT	2.4	2.1	2.1
KEPI	2.8	2.5	2.9
KEEP	2.4	2.2	2.3
KELY	2.5	2.4	2.8
KENE	3.7	3.5	4.1
KETE	4.8	4.1	4.8
KILT	1.7	1.4	1.5
KILL	1.1	1.0	1.0
KISS	2.3	2.1	2.2
KIDU	4.5	4.2	4.5
KINE	3.3	3.2	3.2
KOPA	2.3	2.5	1.8
KOLD	7.4	7.5	6.1
KOPS	6.8	6.7	6.4
KOOK	2.1	2.3	1.9
KOLI	2.0	2.3	1.3
KUTE	8.7	8.3	9.2

STUDY 6 :   SURVEY OF ORGANISATIONAL BUYING PROCESSES - KOREX MARKET
****

Survey based on interviews with 20 companies. Numbers
below represent the estimated relative weight of
different decision makers in the buying decisions.

| | AGGREGATE | GEOGRAPHICAL SEGMENTATION | | |
		EAST	CENTRAL	WEST
PRODUCTION MANAGER	23.98	24.37	23.87	23.85
ENGINEERING MANAGER	39.65	39.23	40.00	39.62
PURCHASING MANAGER	19.02	19.02	18.87	19.12
GENERAL MANAGER	17.36	17.38	17.26	17.41

STUDY 7 : SEMANTIC SCALES ON PRODUCT PERCEPTION - KOREX MARKET
****

Survey based on interviews with 50 companies. Three dimensions
were found to be of determinant importance in explaining the
perceptions of products :

      DIMENSION 1 : PRICE (PRI)
      DIMENSION 2 : RESISTANCE (RES)
      DIMENSION 3 : SUSPENSION (SUS)

              * RELATIVE IMPORTANCE OF DIMENSIONS
              =====================================

              Relative weight for each dimension.
              (Sum over the three dimensions is equal to 100).

	AGGREGATE				EAST				GEOGRAPHICAL SEGMENTATION CENTRAL				WEST			
	PRO	ENG	PUR	GAL	PRO	ENG	PUR	GAL	PRO	ENG	PUR	GAL	PRO	ENG	PUR	GAL
PRI	36.	24.	62.	40.	36.	24.	62.	40.	36.	24.	63.	40.	35.	24.	62.	40.
RES	33.	42.	17.	30.	33.	43.	17.	30.	33.	42.	17.	30.	33.	42.	17.	30.
SUS	31.	33.	21.	30.	31.	33.	21.	30.	31.	33.	20.	30.	31.	33.	21.	30.

              * IDEAL POINTS
              ==============

              Most desired combination on 1-7 scales.
              (1 = low, 7 = high)

	AGGREGATE				EAST				GEOGRAPHICAL SEGMENTATION CENTRAL				WEST			
	PRO	ENG	PUR	GAL	PRO	ENG	PUR	GAL	PRO	ENG	PUR	GAL	PRO	ENG	PUR	GAL
PRI	3.1	3.5	3.2	2.8	3.1	3.8	3.0	3.4	3.1	4.2	2.9	3.0	3.1	3.7	3.2	2.9
RES	4.8	4.2	4.0	3.9	4.6	4.4	4.3	4.0	4.1	4.6	4.1	4.1	4.7	4.3	3.8	4.2
SUS	4.9	5.4	4.8	4.2	4.9	5.6	4.6	4.2	4.7	5.4	4.3	4.1	5.5	4.8	4.6	4.4

* PERCEPTIONS OF PRODUCTS
===========================
Perceptions on 1-7 scales.
(1 = low, 7 = high)

.   PRICE   .
_____

	AGGREGATE				EAST				GEOGRAPHICAL SEGMENTATION CENTRAL				WEST			
	PRO	ENG	PUR	GAL	PRO	ENG	PUR	GAL	PRO	ENG	PUR	GAL	PRO	ENG	PUR	GAL
KALA	4.	4.	4.	4.	4.	4.	4.	4.	4.	4.	4.	4.	4.	4.	4.	4.
KAST	5.	4.	4.	4.	5.	5.	4.	5.	5.	5.	4.	5.	4.	4.	5.	5.
KAMI	4.	3.	4.	4.	4.	3.	3.	4.	3.	4.	3.	3.	3.	4.	3.	3.
KAPE	4.	4.	4.	4.	4.	5.	4.	4.	4.	4.	5.	4.	4.	4.	4.	5.
KAMO	4.	3.	3.	3.	3.	4.	4.	4.	4.	3.	3.	3.	3.	4.	4.	4.
KAMU	3.	4.	4.	4.	3.	3.	3.	3.	3.	4.	3.	3.	3.	4.	3.	4.
KAPI	4.	4.	4.	4.	4.	4.	4.	4.	4.	4.	4.	4.	4.	4.	4.	4.
KENT	6.	6.	6.	6.	6.	6.	6.	6.	6.	7.	6.	7.	6.	6.	7.	6.
KEPI	5.	5.	5.	5.	5.	5.	5.	5.	5.	5.	5.	5.	5.	5.	4.	5.
KEEP	5.	5.	4.	5.	5.	5.	4.	5.	4.	4.	4.	4.	5.	4.	4.	5.
KELY	3.	3.	3.	3.	3.	3.	4.	3.	3.	3.	4.	3.	3.	4.	3.	3.
KENE	3.	4.	3.	3.	3.	4.	3.	3.	3.	3.	3.	3.	4.	4.	3.	3.
KETE	3.	3.	4.	3.	4.	4.	4.	4.	4.	4.	4.	4.	4.	3.	4.	3.
KILT	2.	2.	3.	2.	2.	2.	3.	2.	2.	2.	2.	2.	2.	2.	3.	2.
KILL	2.	2.	3.	3.	3.	3.	3.	3.	3.	3.	3.	3.	3.	3.	3.	2.
KISS	3.	3.	3.	3.	3.	3.	3.	3.	3.	3.	3.	3.	3.	3.	3.	3.
KIDU	4.	4.	3.	3.	3.	3.	3.	3.	3.	3.	4.	3.	3.	4.	3.	3.
KINE	3.	4.	4.	3.	3.	3.	3.	3.	3.	4.	3.	3.	3.	4.	4.	3.
KOPA	5.	5.	4.	5.	5.	5.	5.	5.	4.	5.	5.	5.	5.	5.	5.	4.
KOLD	3.	3.	3.	3.	3.	3.	3.	3.	3.	3.	3.	3.	4.	3.	3.	3.
KOPS	3.	4.	4.	4.	4.	4.	4.	4.	4.	3.	4.	4.	4.	4.	4.	4.
KOOK	5.	4.	5.	5.	5.	5.	5.	4.	4.	4.	5.	5.	5.	5.	5.	5.
KOLI	4.	4.	4.	4.	3.	4.	3.	3.	4.	4.	3.	3.	4.	3.	3.	3.
KUTE	4.	4.	3.	3.	4.	4.	4.	3.	4.	3.	4.	4.	3.	4.	3.	3.

. RESISTANCE .

	AGGREGATE				EAST				GEOGRAPHICAL SEGMENTATION CENTRAL				WEST			
	PRO	ENG	PUR	GAL	PRO	ENG	PUR	GAL	PRO	ENG	PUR	GAL	PRO	ENG	PUR	GAL
KALA	6.	6.	6.	6.	7.	6.	7.	6.	7.	7.	6.	6.	6.	6.	6.	6.
KAST	2.	2.	2.	2.	2.	2.	2.	1.	2.	2.	2.	2.	2.	2.	2.	2.
KAMI	4.	5.	4.	4.	4.	4.	4.	5.	4.	4.	4.	5.	4.	4.	5.	4.
KAPE	2.	2.	2.	2.	2.	2.	2.	2.	2.	2.	2.	2.	2.	2.	2.	2.
KAMO	3.	3.	3.	3.	3.	3.	3.	3.	3.	3.	3.	3.	3.	4.	3.	3.
KAMU	4.	4.	3.	4.	4.	4.	3.	3.	4.	4.	4.	4.	4.	4.	4.	4.
KAPI	3.	3.	3.	3.	3.	3.	3.	3.	3.	3.	3.	3.	3.	3.	3.	3.
KENT	3.	3.	3.	3.	3.	3.	3.	3.	3.	3.	3.	3.	3.	3.	3.	3.
KEPI	3.	3.	3.	3.	3.	3.	3.	3.	3.	3.	3.	3.	3.	3.	3.	3.
KEEP	2.	3.	3.	2.	3.	3.	3.	2.	3.	2.	3.	2.	3.	3.	2.	3.
KELY	2.	2.	2.	2.	2.	2.	2.	2.	2.	2.	2.	2.	2.	2.	2.	2.
KENE	3.	3.	3.	2.	2.	2.	3.	2.	2.	3.	3.	2.	3.	2.	3.	2.
KETE	4.	3.	4.	3.	3.	3.	3.	3.	3.	3.	3.	3.	3.	3.	3.	3.
KILT	2.	2.	2.	2.	3.	2.	2.	2.	2.	2.	2.	2.	2.	2.	2.	2.
KILL	2.	2.	2.	2.	3.	2.	2.	2.	2.	3.	3.	2.	3.	3.	2.	2.
KISS	4.	3.	4.	3.	4.	4.	3.	3.	3.	3.	3.	3.	3.	4.	3.	3.
KIDU	4.	4.	4.	4.	4.	4.	4.	4.	4.	4.	4.	4.	4.	4.	4.	4.
KINE	2.	2.	2.	2.	2.	2.	2.	2.	2.	2.	3.	2.	2.	2.	3.	2.
KOPA	3.	3.	3.	3.	3.	3.	3.	3.	3.	3.	3.	3.	3.	3.	3.	3.
KOLD	4.	4.	4.	4.	4.	4.	4.	4.	4.	4.	4.	4.	4.	4.	4.	4.
KOPS	4.	4.	4.	4.	4.	4.	4.	4.	4.	4.	4.	4.	4.	4.	4.	4.
KOOK	3.	2.	3.	2.	3.	3.	2.	2.	3.	3.	3.	2.	3.	3.	2.	3.
KOLI	3.	3.	2.	3.	3.	3.	3.	3.	3.	3.	3.	2.	2.	3.	2.	3.
KUTE	4.	4.	4.	4.	4.	4.	4.	4.	4.	4.	4.	4.	4.	4.	4.	4.

.   SUSPENSION   .

	AGGREGATE				EAST				GEOGRAPHICAL SEGMENTATION CENTRAL				WEST			
	PRO	ENG	PUR	GAL	PRO	ENG	PUR	GAL	PRO	ENG	PUR	GAL	PRO	ENG	PUR	GAL
KALA	3.	4.	3.	4.	3.	3.	3.	3.	4.	4.	3.	3.	3.	4.	3.	3.
KAST	2.	2.	2.	2.	2.	2.	2.	2.	2.	2.	2.	2.	2.	2.	2.	2.
KAMI	3.	3.	3.	3.	3.	3.	3.	3.	4.	3.	3.	3.	3.	3.	3.	3.
KAPE	3.	4.	3.	3.	3.	3.	3.	3.	4.	4.	3.	3.	4.	4.	3.	3.
KAMO	4.	4.	4.	3.	4.	4.	4.	4.	4.	4.	4.	4.	4.	4.	4.	4.
KAMU	4.	4.	4.	4.	4.	4.	4.	4.	4.	4.	4.	4.	5.	4.	4.	4.
KAPI	3.	4.	4.	3.	3.	4.	3.	3.	3.	4.	3.	3.	3.	4.	3.	3.
KENT	4.	4.	4.	4.	4.	4.	4.	4.	4.	4.	4.	4.	4.	4.	4.	4.
KEPI	4.	4.	3.	3.	4.	4.	4.	4.	3.	3.	3.	3.	4.	4.	3.	3.
KEEP	3.	3.	3.	3.	3.	3.	3.	3.	3.	3.	3.	3.	3.	3.	3.	3.
KELY	4.	4.	4.	3.	4.	4.	4.	3.	4.	4.	3.	3.	3.	4.	3.	4.
KENE	5.	5.	5.	5.	5.	5.	5.	5.	5.	5.	5.	5.	5.	6.	6.	5.
KETE	6.	6.	5.	5.	6.	5.	6.	6.	5.	6.	5.	6.	6.	5.	5.	6.
KILT	6.	6.	7.	7.	6.	7.	7.	6.	7.	6.	6.	7.	7.	6.	6.	6.
KILL	4.	4.	4.	4.	4.	4.	4.	4.	4.	4.	4.	4.	4.	4.	4.	4.
KISS	3.	3.	3.	3.	3.	2.	3.	2.	3.	3.	3.	2.	3.	2.	3.	2.
KIDU	4.	4.	4.	4.	4.	3.	4.	3.	4.	4.	4.	4.	4.	4.	4.	4.
KINE	6.	6.	6.	6.	5.	5.	6.	6.	5.	5.	6.	5.	6.	6.	6.	5.
KOPA	2.	3.	2.	2.	3.	2.	3.	3.	3.	3.	3.	3.	2.	3.	2.	2.
KOLD	4.	4.	4.	4.	4.	4.	4.	4.	4.	4.	3.	4.	4.	4.	4.	4.
KOPS	4.	4.	3.	3.	4.	4.	4.	4.	4.	4.	4.	4.	4.	4.	3.	3.
KOOK	3.	3.	3.	3.	3.	3.	3.	3.	3.	3.	3.	3.	3.	3.	3.	3.
KOLI	4.	4.	4.	4.	4.	4.	4.	4.	4.	4.	4.	4.	4.	4.	4.	4.
KUTE	5.	5.	5.	5.	5.	6.	6.	5.	6.	5.	5.	5.	5.	5.	6.	6.

STUDY 8 :   PERCEPTUAL MAP OF PRODUCTS - KOREX MARKET
****

Study based on interviews with 20 companies.

Data gathering and analysis based on a non-
metric multidimensional scaling methodology.

A maximum of 20 products is used in this study.
If more products are on the market, only
the first 20 with the largest volume sale
are considered in this map.
Information on others may be found in study 7.

No significant statistical difference was
observed between the perceptions of different
decision makers.

Perceptual scales from - 20 to + 20.

```
                              * AGGREGATE MARKET ANALYSIS
                              ============================

                         The two most important dimensions in
                         explaining client product preferences are  :

                         1 - Horizontal axis (increasing to the right)  :  PRICE
                         2 - Vertical axis (increasing to the top)  :  RESISTANCE
                                                     -
                                                     :
                                                     :
                                                     :
                                                     :
                                                     -
                                                     :
                                                     P
                                                     :
                                                     :
                                                     -
                                                     :
                                                     :
                                                     :
                                                     :
                                                     -
                                                     :
                                                     :
                                               1   2:
                                               3 F :
                         :----:----:----4*C-B:----:----:----:----:
                                               T   :
                                                   :
                                                   :
                                               M   :
                                               !  -
                                                   :    JR           N
                                                   :
                                                   :
                                                   :    L
                             Q         +    -    O
                                                   :
                                                   :
                                                   :
                                               I   :
                                                  -S
                                                   :
                                                   :
                                                   :
                                                   :
                                                   -

           SUPERIMPOSED POINTS IN GRAPH  :  * FOR  :  A D
                                            + FOR  :  E G
                                            ! FOR  :  H K
```

* IDEAL POINTS *	DEC MAKERS *	COORD.AXIS1 *	COORD.AXIS2 *
*	*	*	*
1	PRO	-4.5	2.8
2	ENG	-1.1	2.5
3	PUR	-5.5	1.7
4	GAL	-5.7	0.5

* PERCEPTION *	PRODUCTS *	COORD.AXIS1 *	COORD.AXIS2 *
*	*	*	*
A	KOLD	-4.6	-0.4
B	KOPS	-1.8	-0.4
C	KUTE	-3.6	-0.1
D	KIDU	-4.7	-0.8
E	KENE	-4.4	-10.2
F	KAMI	-3.9	1.7
G	KINE	-4.6	-10.3
H	KAMO	-2.2	-5.4
I	KELY	-4.2	-14.8
J	KEPI	4.9	-6.2
K	KETE	-2.1	-5.1
L	KEEP	4.2	-9.9
M	KISS	-5.5	-4.4
N	KENT	15.1	-6.9
O	KOOK	4.5	-10.1
P	KALA	-0.1	14.0
Q	KILT	-11.2	-11.0
R	KOPA	5.1	-6.6
S	KAPE	1.5	-15.3
T	KAMU	-3.0	-1.9

```
                * GEOGRAPHICAL MARKET ANALYSIS  :  EAST
                ==========================================

          The two most important dimensions in
          explaining client product preferences are  :

          1 - Horizontal axis (increasing to the right) :  PRICE
          2 - Vertical axis (increasing to the top)  :  RESISTANCE
                                                -
                                                :
                                                :
                                                :
                                                :
                                                R
                                                :
                                                :
                                                :
                                                :
                                                -
                                                :
                                                :
                                                :
                                                :
                                                -
                                                :
                                    1           :
                                    G 2:
                                 3          :
          :----:----:----:----*DC-B:----:----:----:----:
                                                :
                                    T :
                                                :
                                M   I :
                                    K -
                                                :         +
                                                :                        N
                                                :
                                                :      P
                                    E   -   L
                            O                   :
                                    F   :
                                    H   :
                                                :S
                                                -
                                                :
                                                :
                                                :
                                                :
                                                -


          SUPERIMPOSED POINTS IN GRAPH  :   * FOR  :   4 A
                                            + FOR  :   J Q
```

* IDEAL POINTS *	DEC MAKERS *	COORD.AXIS1 *	COORD.AXIS2 *
1	PRO	-4.3	3.0
2	ENG	-1.3	2.8
3	PUR	-6.6	1.6
4	GAL	-5.6	0.5

* PERCEPTION *	PRODUCTS *	COORD.AXIS1 *	COORD.AXIS2 *
A	KOLD	-5.3	-0.4
B	KOPS	-1.7	-0.5
C	KUTE	-3.4	0.0
D	KIDU	-4.4	-0.8
E	KENE	-4.1	-10.2
F	KINE	-4.5	-12.2
G	KAMI	-3.6	2.1
H	KELY	-4.4	-14.0
I	KETE	-2.1	-4.5
J	KEPI	5.6	-6.2
K	KAMO	-2.2	-5.7
L	KEEP	3.5	-10.4
M	KISS	-6.0	-4.5
N	KENT	15.4	-7.5
O	KILT	-11.0	-11.4
P	KOOK	4.2	-10.0
Q	KOPA	5.5	-6.7
R	KALA	-0.1	15.2
S	KAPE	1.5	-14.4
T	KAMU	-3.0	-2.3

```
                    * GEOGRAPHICAL MARKET ANALYSIS  :   CENTRAL
                    =============================================

        The two most important dimensions in
        explaining client product preferences are  :

        1 - Horizontal axis (increasing to the right)  :  PRICE
        2 - Vertical axis (increasing to the top)  :  RESISTANCE
                                          _
                                          :
                                          :
                                          :
                                          :
                                          Q
                                          :
                                          :
                                          :
                                          :
                                          :
                                          —
                                          :
                                          :
                                          :
                                          :
                                          —
                                          :
                                          :
                               1  2:
                               3 F  :
         :————:————:————4*C–B:————:————:————:————:
                               T  :
                               M  :
                                  + —
                                  :     J
                                  :     P              O
                                  :
                               E  :  !
                                  —
                    R        G  :
                               :
                               :
                               :S
                               I  —
                                  :
                                  :
                                  :
                                  :
                                  —



        SUPERIMPOSED POINTS IN GRAPH  :  * FOR  :  A D
                                         + FOR  :  H L
                                         ! FOR  :  K N
```

* IDEAL POINTS *	DEC MAKERS *	COORD.AXIS1 *	COORD.AXIS2 *
1	PRO	-4.4	2.9
2	ENG	-1.3	2.6
3	PUR	-5.5	1.4
4	GAL	-5.5	0.6

* PERCEPTION *	PRODUCTS *	COORD.AXIS1 *	COORD.AXIS2 *
A	KOLD	-4.9	-0.4
B	KOPS	-2.0	-0.4
C	KUTE	-3.5	-0.1
D	KIDU	-4.8	-0.8
E	KENE	-3.9	-9.9
F	KAMI	-3.9	1.7
G	KINE	-4.6	-11.6
H	KAMO	-2.0	-5.5
I	KELY	-4.4	-15.4
J	KEPI	5.6	-6.1
K	KEEP	4.2	-10.0
L	KETE	-2.3	-5.1
M	KISS	-5.9	-3.7
N	KOOK	4.1	-9.1
O	KENT	15.6	-7.8
P	KOPA	5.3	-7.2
Q	KALA	-0.1	15.8
R	KILT	-11.2	-11.9
S	KAPE	1.5	-14.7
T	KAMU	-3.1	-2.0

```
                    * GEOGRAPHICAL MARKET ANALYSIS  :  WEST
                    ==========================================

          The two most important dimensions in
          explaining client product preferences are  :

          1 - Horizontal axis (increasing to the right)  :  PRICE
          2 - Vertical axis (increasing to the top)  :  RESISTANCE
                                                   -
                                                   :
                                                   :
                                                   :
                                                   :
                                                   -
                                                   :
                                                   :
                                                   M
                                                   :
                                                   -
                                                   :
                                                   :
                                                   :
                                                   :
                                                   -
                                                   :
                                                   :
                                        1   2:
                                        3 D   :
          :----:----:---4BEA-C:----:----:----:----:
                                          S   :
                                        N   :
                                          K :
                                          G -
                                          :   J
                                          :                  O
                                          :   T
                                        F -  *
                            Q           H :
                                          :
                                          :
                                        I :P
                                          -
                                          :
                                          :
                                          :
                                          -

          SUPERIMPOSED POINTS IN GRAPH  :  * FOR :  L R
```

* IDEAL POINTS *	DEC MAKERS *	COORD.AXIS1 *	COORD.AXIS2 *
1	PRO	-4.1	2.8
2	ENG	-1.2	2.6
3	PUR	-6.4	1.5
4	GAL	-6.1	0.5

* PERCEPTION *	PRODUCTS *	COORD.AXIS1 *	COORD.AXIS2 *
A	KUTE	-3.2	-0.1
B	KOLD	-5.2	-0.5
C	KOPS	-1.8	-0.5
D	KAMI	-4.0	1.4
E	KIDU	-4.8	-0.8
F	KENE	-4.0	-10.6
G	KAMO	-2.2	-5.6
H	KINE	-4.2	-11.5
I	KELY	-4.0	-14.9
J	KEPI	4.7	-6.9
K	KETE	-2.3	-4.5
L	KEEP	3.8	-10.9
M	KALA	-0.1	12.4
N	KISS	-5.5	-3.9
O	KENT	15.2	-7.6
P	KAPE	1.5	-14.7
Q	KILT	-12.0	-11.6
R	KOOK	4.0	-10.8
S	KAMU	-3.3	-2.1
T	KOPA	5.9	-8.0

STUDY 9 : MARKET FORECAST - KOREX MARKET
****

Estimates based on econometric analysis of historical
data as well as analysis of future market developments.
Estimates based on volume.

	AGGREGATE	GEOGRAPHICAL SEGMENTATION		
		EAST	CENTRAL	WEST
FORECAST FOR NEXT YEAR				
VOLUME	635000.	194000.	305000.	136000.
GROWTH RATE	-2.1	4.1	-4.6	-4.6
FORECAST FOR FIFTH YEAR				
VOLUME	511000.	275000.	178000.	58000.
GROWTH RATE	-4.7	8.1	-11.1	-16.5

STUDY 10 : PRODUCT AWARENESS AND PREFERENCE SURVEY - LOMEX MARKET
****

Telephone survey of 50 companies.

* PRODUCT AWARENESS
===================

Percentage having a satisfactory knowledge of product.

PRODUCT	AGGREGATE				EAST				GEOGRAPHICAL SEGMENTATION CENTRAL				WEST			
	PRO	ENG	PUR	GAL	PRO	ENG	PUR	GAL	PRO	ENG	PUR	GAL	PRO	ENG	PUR	GAL
LIFE	61.	60.	59.	49.	60.	60.	59.	48.	63.	62.	61.	51.	60.	59.	58.	48.
LUVV	64.	65.	65.	57.	64.	65.	65.	57.	62.	63.	64.	56.	65.	66.	65.	58.

* PRODUCT PREFERENCE
====================

Percentage of individuals stating a greater preference for a given product,
weighted by the purchase volume of the corresponding client companies.

PRODUCT	AGGREGATE				EAST				GEOGRAPHICAL SEGMENTATION CENTRAL				WEST			
	PRO	ENG	PUR	GAL	PRO	ENG	PUR	GAL	PRO	ENG	PUR	GAL	PRO	ENG	PUR	GAL
LIFE	82.	64.	84.	88.	77.	61.	81.	88.	84.	66.	83.	90.	85.	65.	87.	86.
LUVV	18.	36.	16.	12.	23.	39.	19.	12.	16.	34.	17.	10.	15.	35.	13.	14.

STUDY 11 : DEMAND ANALYSIS - LOMEX MARKET
****

Estimates based on statistical sources, interviews
in 30 companies and managerial judgment.

		GEOGRAPHICAL SEGMENTATION		
	AGGREGATE	EAST	CENTRAL	WEST
NUMBER OF CLIENTS	10778.	2736.	3224.	4818.
TOTAL VALUE (000 $)	32217.	9107.	10032.	13078.
TOTAL VOLUME (000 UNITS)	73.	21.	23.	29.
AVERAGE/CLIENT (VALUE 000 $)	2989.	3329.	3111.	2714.
AVERAGE/CLIENT (VOLUME 000 UNITS)	7.	8.	7.	6.
PRIMARY SOURCING (% VALUE)	60.	63.	59.	58.
PRIMARY SOURCING (% VOLUME)	80.	81.	80.	79.
AVERAGE NUMBER OF SUPPLIERS PER CLIENT	3.01	3.00	3.03	3.00

STUDY 12 : MARKET SHARES SURVEY - LOMEX MARKET
****

Estimates based on survey of 40 companies.

* AGGREGATE MARKET SHARES
===========================

PRODUCTS	% TESTS	% CLIENTS		% VOLUME			% VALUE		
		SUPPL	PRIM	SUPPL	PRIM	TOTAL	SUPPL	PRIM	TOTAL
LIFE	8.8	12.3	80.1	3.9	81.1	65.4	0.9	48.7	29.6
LUVV	14.1	252.5	19.9	96.1	18.9	34.6	99.1	51.3	70.4

* MARKET SHARES AS PRIMARY SUPPLIER
====================================

	GEOGRAPHICAL SEGMENTATION					
	EAST		CENTRAL		WEST	
PRODUCTS	% VOL	% VAL	% VOL	% VAL	% VOL	% VAL
LIFE	79.2	45.8	82.4	51.1	81.3	49.1
LUVV	20.8	54.2	17.6	48.9	18.7	50.9

* MARKET SHARES AS SUPPLEMENTARY SUPPLIER
==

	GEOGRAPHICAL SEGMENTATION					
	EAST		CENTRAL		WEST	
PRODUCTS	% VOL	% VAL	% VOL	% VAL	% VOL	% VAL
LIFE	6.0	1.4	5.2	1.2	1.6	0.4
LUVV	94.0	98.6	94.8	98.8	98.4	99.6

* MARKET SHARES TOTALS
========================

	GEOGRAPHICAL SEGMENTATION					
	EAST		CENTRAL		WEST	
PRODUCTS	% VOL	% VAL	% VOL	% VAL	% VOL	% VAL
LIFE	65.3	29.5	66.8	30.9	64.3	28.6
LUVV	34.7	70.5	33.2	69.1	35.7	71.4

* PROPORTION OF PRODUCTS IN TESTS
==================================

	GEOGRAPHICAL SEGMENTATION		
PRODUCTS	EAST	CENTRAL	WEST
LIFE	9.6	13.3	5.3
LUVV	14.0	11.8	15.8

STUDY 13 :   SURVEY OF ORGANISATIONAL BUYING PROCESSES - LOMEX MARKET
****

Survey based on interviews with 20 companies.
Numbers below represent the estimated relative
weight of different decision makers in the buying decisions.

| | AGGREGATE | GEOGRAPHICAL SEGMENTATION | | |
		EAST	CENTRAL	WEST
PRODUCTION MANAGER	19.91	20.03	19.95	19.82
ENGINEERING MANAGER	21.18	21.17	20.93	21.36
PURCHASING MANAGER	18.85	18.86	18.57	19.04
GENERAL MANAGER	40.05	39.94	40.55	39.79

STUDY 14 : SEMANTIC SCALES ON PRODUCT PERCEPTION - LOMEX MARKET
****

Survey based on interviews with 50 companies. Three dimensions
were found to be of determinant importance in explaining the
perceptions of products :

     DIMENSION 1 : PRICE (PRI)
     DIMENSION 2 : CONVEXITY (COV)
     DIMENSION 3 : CONDUCTIVITY (COD)

* RELATIVE IMPORTANCE OF DIMENSIONS
=====================================

Relative weight for each dimension.
(Sum over the three dimensions is equal to 100).

GEOGRAPHICAL SEGMENTATION

	AGGREGATE				EAST				CENTRAL				WEST			
	PRO	ENG	PUR	GAL	PRO	ENG	PUR	GAL	PRO	ENG	PUR	GAL	PRO	ENG	PUR	GAL
PRI	34.	36.	26.	44.	34.	36.	26.	44.	34.	36.	26.	44.	34.	36.	26.	44.
COV	36.	49.	16.	32.	36.	49.	16.	32.	36.	49.	16.	32.	36.	48.	16.	32.
COD	30.	16.	59.	23.	30.	15.	59.	23.	30.	15.	59.	23.	30.	16.	59.	24.

* IDEAL POINTS
==============

Most desired combination on 1-7 scales.
(1 = low, 7 = high)

GEOGRAPHICAL SEGMENTATION

	AGGREGATE				EAST				CENTRAL				WEST			
	PRO	ENG	PUR	GAL	PRO	ENG	PUR	GAL	PRO	ENG	PUR	GAL	PRO	ENG	PUR	GAL
PRI	2.8	3.6	2.0	1.5	2.8	3.8	2.0	1.6	2.4	3.8	1.9	1.5	2.7	4.0	1.9	1.5
COV	3.9	3.8	4.1	4.2	3.8	3.7	3.6	3.9	4.0	3.8	3.8	4.3	4.3	3.7	4.2	3.9
COD	4.2	4.6	3.3	3.5	4.1	4.9	3.1	3.3	4.3	5.2	3.3	3.8	4.0	4.6	3.4	3.2

```
                    * PERCEPTIONS OF PRODUCTS
                    ==========================

                    Perceptions on 1-7 scales.
                    (1 = low, 7 = high)
```

```
                          .      PRICE       .
                          ---------------------
```

		AGGREGATE				EAST			GEOGRAPHICAL SEGMENTATION CENTRAL				WEST			
	PRO	ENG	PUR	GAL	PRO	ENG	PUR	GAL	PRO	ENG	PUR	GAL	PRO	ENG	PUR	GAL
LIFE	3.	4.	2.	1.	3.	4.	2.	1.	3.	4.	2.	1.	3.	4.	2.	1.
LUVV	1.	1.	0.	0.	1.	1.	0.	0.	2.	2.	0.	0.	2.	1.	0.	1.

```
                          .    CONVEXITY     .
                          ---------------------
```

		AGGREGATE				EAST			GEOGRAPHICAL SEGMENTATION CENTRAL				WEST			
	PRO	ENG	PUR	GAL	PRO	ENG	PUR	GAL	PRO	ENG	PUR	GAL	PRO	ENG	PUR	GAL
LIFE	4.	4.	4.	4.	4.	4.	4.	4.	4.	4.	4.	4.	4.	4.	4.	4.
LUVV	4.	5.	5.	4.	5.	4.	5.	5.	4.	4.	4.	5.	4.	5.	5.	4.

```
                          .   CONDUCTIVITY   .
                          ---------------------
```

		AGGREGATE				EAST			GEOGRAPHICAL SEGMENTATION CENTRAL				WEST			
	PRO	ENG	PUR	GAL	PRO	ENG	PUR	GAL	PRO	ENG	PUR	GAL	PRO	ENG	PUR	GAL
LIFE	4.	5.	4.	4.	4.	5.	3.	4.	5.	5.	3.	4.	5.	5.	3.	4.
LUVV	4.	5.	2.	3.	4.	5.	2.	3.	4.	4.	3.	3.	4.	5.	2.	3.

STUDY 15 :   MARKET FORECAST – LOMEX MARKET
****

Estimates based on econometric analysis
of historical data as well as analysis
of future market developments.
Estimates based on volume.

| | AGGREGATE | GEOGRAPHICAL SEGMENTATION | | |
		EAST	CENTRAL	WEST
FORECAST FOR NEXT YEAR				
VOLUME	96000.	28000.	32000.	36000.
GROWTH RATE	32.0	37.1	37.1	24.6
FORECAST FOR FIFTH YEAR				
VOLUME	170000.	62000.	70000.	39000.
GROWTH RATE	18.4	24.5	24.5	6.3

STUDY 16 : COMPETITIVE INFORMATION
****

Estimates obtained from a variety of sources.

* AGGREGATE PRODUCT MANAGEMENT INFORMATION
===

PRODUCTS	MAXIMUM PRICE DISCOUNT (%)	PROMOTION (000$)	SALES COMMISSION (%)	TECHNICAL SUPPORT (000$)	PRODUCT ADVERTISING (000$)
KALA	10.7	0.	4.7	82.	0.
KAST	9.4	0.	5.2	82.	0.
KAMI	10.8	96.	7.3	484.	98.
KAPE	9.3	0.	4.7	314.	0.
KAMO	5.0	156.	10.6	310.	99.
KAMU	4.6	103.	9.5	151.	103.
KAPI	5.1	103.	10.1	156.	52.
KENT	3.9	311.	3.1	210.	53.
KEPI	4.4	98.	2.0	240.	47.
KEEP	3.9	102.	3.3	218.	52.
KELY	4.0	272.	2.0	226.	47.
KENE	3.8	589.	3.8	321.	109.
KETE	4.1	388.	3.9	301.	98.
LIFE	9.3	653.	7.0	527.	98.
KILT	4.9	76.	5.2	137.	2.
KILL	4.9	104.	4.5	182.	18.
KISS	5.4	201.	5.2	184.	17.
KIDU	9.7	205.	4.9	413.	16.
KINE	4.7	277.	5.2	380.	16.
KOPA	5.0	20.	3.7	155.	20.
KOLD	3.1	266.	6.2	682.	246.
KOPS	2.8	162.	3.7	542.	309.
KOOK	3.6	23.	3.9	180.	9.
KOLI	4.7	104.	6.0	180.	104.
KUTE	11.0	27.	9.2	509.	27.
LUVV	10.8	264.	10.3	531.	100.

* CORPORATE INFORMATION
========================

| | FIRMS | | | | |
	1	2	3	4	5
SALES FORCE					
NB OF SALESPERSONS	97.	65.	83.	116.	25.
TRAINING EXPENDITURE	49.	178.	192.	73.	26.
(000$)					
TECHNICAL FORCE					
NB OF TECHNICIANS	39.	37.	40.	42.	25.
TRAINING EXPENDITURE	16.	93.	141.	46.	26.
(000$)					
CORPORATE MARKETING	53.	50.	0.	46.	20.
(000$)					

* ALLOCATION OF SALES AND TECHNICAL FORCES
===

ON BASIS OF DECISION-MAKERS

	SALES FORCE				TECHNICAL FORCE			
FIRM	PRO	ENG	PUR	GAL	PRO	ENG	PUR	GAL
1	0.40	0.40	0.10	0.10	0.39	0.61	0.00	0.00
2	0.25	0.34	0.25	0.16	0.42	0.58	0.00	0.00
3	0.30	0.24	0.29	0.18	0.45	0.45	0.05	0.05
4	0.19	0.30	0.25	0.25	0.40	0.50	0.10	0.00
5	0.25	0.25	0.25	0.25	0.25	0.25	0.25	0.24

ON BASIS OF GEOGRAPHICAL SEGMENTATION

	SALES FORCE			TECHNICAL FORCE		
FIRM	EAST	CENTRAL	WEST	EAST	CENTRAL	WEST
1	0.27	0.33	0.40	0.27	0.34	0.39
2	0.34	0.33	0.33	0.34	0.33	0.33
3	0.30	0.40	0.30	0.30	0.40	0.30
4	0.35	0.45	0.20	0.35	0.45	0.20
5	0.33	0.33	0.34	0.33	0.33	0.34

appendix C

Blank Forms

This appendix contains twelve blank copies of the decision form, the budgeting form, and the planning form. They are to be detached and filled in as needed in the course of the simulation.

INDUSTRAT DECISION FORM

Firm : _____   Industry : _____

Number of products for sale : _____   Period : _____

Number of development projects : _____

Number of new projects licensed out : _____

Number of new projects licensed in : _____

PRODUCT MANAGEMENT

	Product Name	Development Project (New/Mod Product Only)	Production ('000s)	List Price ($)	Maximum Price Discount (%)	Sales Force Commission (%)	Promotion ($'000)	Product Advertising ($'000)	Allocation of Technical Support (%)
2									
3									
4									
5									
6									
7									
8									
9									
10									
11									100 %

SALES FORCE MANAGEMENT

12 Organizational Structure (code) [   ]   Total Number of Salespersons [   ]   Sales Force Training ($'000) [   ]

ALLOCATION (%)

13 Geography	E	C	W	100 %
14 Size	S	M	L	100 %
15 End Product	I	CN	CR	100 %
16 DMU	P	E	PU	G	100 %

TECHNICAL FORCE MANAGEMENT

17 Total Number of Technicians [   ]   Tech. Force Training ($'000) [   ]

ALLOCATION (%)

18 Geography	E	C	W	100 %
19 Size	S	M	L	100 %
20 End Product	I	CN	CR	100 %
21 DMU	P	E	PU	G	100 %

CORPORATE MARKETING

22 Corporate Communications ($'000) [   ]

RESEARCH AND DEVELOPMENT

Research

	Technology (Code)	Investment ($'000)
23		

Development

	Project Name (P . . .)	Technology (Code)	Budget ($'000)	1	2	3	4	Base Cost ($)
				Physical Characteristics				
24								
25								
26								
27								

NEW LICENSING OUT

	Project Name (P . . .)	To Firm (Nº)	Minimum Annual Fee ($'000)
29			
30			
31			
32			
33			

NEW LICENSING IN

	Project Name (P . . .)	From Firm (Nº)	Minimum Annual Fee ($'000)
34			
35			

MARKET RESEARCH STUDIES (Codes)

1	2	3	4	5	6	7	8	9	10	11	12	13	14	15	16
28															

ADMINISTRATIVE ADJUSTMENTS ($'000)

36		
	EC (−) EP (+)	BD (−) BI (+)

MODIFICATIONS RESULTING FROM NEGOTIATIONS BETWEEN
THE FIRM AND THE GAME ADMINISTRATOR

Source of Modification	Exceptional Profits (+) or Costs (—) ($'000)	Budget Increase (+) or Decrease (—) ($'000)
1. Additional information bought from the game administrator		
2. Payment to the Production Department by INDUSTRAT administration for liquidation of obsolete inventory		
Brand x Quantity ('000) x Manufacturing Cost x Proportion (%)		
_____ x _____ x _____ x _____		
_____ x _____ x _____ x _____		
_____ x _____ x _____ x _____		
3. Changes in Marketing Expenditure Budget		
4. Fines		
5. Other Modifications		
TOTAL		

Signature of the firm's representative _____

Signature of the game administrator _____

INDUSTRAT DECISION FORM

Firm : _____   Industry : _____

Number of products for sale : _____   Period : _____

Number of development projects : _____

Number of new projects licensed out : _____

Number of new projects licensed in : _____

PRODUCT MANAGEMENT

	Product Name	Development Project (New/Mod Product Only)	Production ('000s)	List Price ($)	Maximum Price Discount (%)	Sales Force Commission (%)	Promotion ($'000)	Product Advertising ($'000)	Allocation of Technical Support (%)
2									
3									
4									
5									
6									
7									
8									
9									
10									
11									100 %

SALES FORCE MANAGEMENT

12 Organizational Structure (code) [ ]   Total Number of Salespersons [ ]   Sales Force Training ($'000) [ ]

ALLOCATION (%)

	E	C	W	
13 Geography				100 %
14 Size	S	M	L	100 %
15 End Product	I	CN	CR	100 %
16 DMU	P	E	PU	G	100 %

TECHNICAL FORCE MANAGEMENT

17 Total Number of Technicians [ ]   Tech. Force Training ($'000) [ ]

ALLOCATION (%)

	E	C	W	
18 Geography				100 %
19 Size	S	M	L	100 %
20 End Product	I	CN	CR	100 %
21 DMU	P	E	PU	G	100 %

CORPORATE MARKETING

22 Corporate Communications ($'000) [ ]

RESEARCH AND DEVELOPMENT

Research

	Technology (Code)	Investment ($'000)
23	[ ]	[ ]

Development

	Project Name (P...)	Technology (Code)	Budget ($'000)	1	Physical Characteristics 2	3	4	Base Cost ($)
24								
25								
26								
27								

NEW LICENSING OUT

	Project Name (P...)	To Firm (N°)	Minimum Annual Fee ($'000)
29			
30			
31			
32			
33			

NEW LICENSING IN

	Project Name (P...)	From Firm (N°)	Minimum Annual Fee ($'000)
34			
35			

MARKET RESEARCH STUDIES (Codes)

	1	2	3	4	5	6	7	8	9	10	11	12	13	14	15	16
28																

ADMINISTRATIVE ADJUSTMENTS ($'000)

	EC (—) EP (+)	BD (—) BI (+)
36		

MODIFICATIONS RESULTING FROM NEGOTIATIONS BETWEEN
THE FIRM AND THE GAME ADMINISTRATOR

Source of Modification	Exceptional Profits (+) or Costs (—) ($'000)	Budget Increase (+) or Decrease (—) ($'000)
1. Additional information bought from the game administrator		
2. Payment to the Production Department by INDUSTRAT administration for liquidation of obsolete inventory		
Brand x Quantity ('000) x Manufacturing Cost x Proportion (%)		
_____ x _____ x _____ x _____		
_____ x _____ x _____ x _____		
_____ x _____ x _____ x _____		
3. Changes in Marketing Expenditure Budget		
4. Fines		
5. Other Modifications		
TOTAL		

Signature of the firm's representative _____

Signature of the game administrator _____

INDUSTRAT DECISION FORM

Firm : _____   Industry : _____

Number of products for sale : _____   Period : _____

Number of development projects : _____

Number of new projects licensed out : _____

Number of new projects licensed in : _____

PRODUCT MANAGEMENT

	Product Name	Development Project (New/Mod Product Only)	Production ('000s)	List Price ($)	Maximum Price Discount (%)	Sales Force Commission (%)	Promotion ($'000)	Product Advertising ($'000)	Allocation of Technical Support (%)
2									
3									
4									
5									
6									
7									
8									
9									
10									
11									100 %

SALES FORCE MANAGEMENT

12 Organizational Structure (code) [   ]   Total Number of Salespersons [   ]   Sales Force Training ($'000) [   ]

ALLOCATION (%)

13 Geography	E	C	W	100 %
14 Size	S	M	L	100 %
15 End Product	I	CN	CR	100 %
16 DMU	P	E	PU	G	100 %

TECHNICAL FORCE MANAGEMENT

17 Total Number of Technicians [   ]   Tech. Force Training ($'000) [   ]

ALLOCATION (%)

18 Geography	E	C	W	100 %
19 Size	S	M	L	100 %
20 End Product	I	CN	CR	100 %
21 DMU	P	E	PU	G	100 %

CORPORATE MARKETING

22 Corporate Communications ($'000) [   ]

RESEARCH AND DEVELOPMENT

Research

	Technology (Code)	Investment ($'000)
23	[ ]	[ ]

Development

	Project Name (P. . . .)	Technology (Code)	Budget ($'000)	Physical Characteristics 1	2	3	4	Base Cost ($)
24								
25								
26								
27								

NEW LICENSING OUT

	Project Name (P. . . .)	To Firm (N°)	Minimum Annual Fee ($'000)
29			
30			
31			
32			
33			

NEW LICENSING IN

	Project Name (P. . . .)	From Firm (N°)	Minimum Annual Fee ($'000)
34			
35			

MARKET RESEARCH STUDIES (Codes)

1	2	3	4	5	6	7	8	9	10	11	12	13	14	15	16
28 | | | | | | | | | | | | | | | | |

ADMINISTRATIVE ADJUSTMENTS ($'000)

36 [   ] [   ]

EC (—) EP (+)   BD (—) BI (+)

MODIFICATIONS RESULTING FROM NEGOTIATIONS BETWEEN
THE FIRM AND THE GAME ADMINISTRATOR

Source of Modification	Exceptional Profits (+) or Costs (—) ($'000)	Budget Increase (+) or Decrease (—) ($'000)
1. Additional information bought from the game administrator		
2. Payment to the Production Department by INDUSTRAT administration for liquidation of obsolete inventory		
3. Changes in Marketing Expenditure Budget		
4. Fines		
5. Other Modifications		
TOTAL		

In section 2:

Brand   x   Quantity ('000)   x   Manufacturing Cost   x   Proportion (%)

_____ x _____ x _____ x _____

_____ x _____ x _____ x _____

_____ x _____ x _____ x _____

Signature of the firm's representative _____

Signature of the game administrator _____

INDUSTRAT DECISION FORM

Firm : _____

Number of products for sale : _____

Number of development projects : _____

Number of new projects licensed out : _____

Number of new projects licensed in : _____

Industry : _____

Period : _____

PRODUCT MANAGEMENT

Product Name	Development Project (Modified Product Only)	Production ('000s)	List Price ($)	Maximum Price Discount (%)	Sales Force Commission (%)	Promotion ($'000)	Product Advertising ($'000)	Allocation of Technical Support (%)
2								
3								
4								
5								
6								
7								
8								
9								
10								
11								100 %

SALES FORCE MANAGEMENT

12 Organizational Structure (code) [ ]   Total Number of Salespersons [ ]   Sales Force Training ($'000) [ ]

ALLOCATION (%)

13 Geography

E	C	W	100 %

14 Size

S	M	L	100 %

15 End Product

I	CN	CR	100 %

16 DMU

P	E	PU	G	100 %

TECHNICAL FORCE MANAGEMENT

17 Total Number of Technicians [ ]   Tech. Force Training ($'000) [ ]

ALLOCATION (%)

18 Geography

E	C	W	100 %

19 Size

S	M	L	100 %

20 End Product

I	CN	CR	100 %

21 DMU

P	E	PU	G	100 %

CORPORATE MARKETING

22 Corporate Communications ($'000) [ ]

RESEARCH AND DEVELOPMENT

Research

Technology (Code)	Investment ($'000)
23 [ ]	[ ]

Development

	Project Name (P....)	Technology (Code)	Budget ($'000)	1	2	3	4	Base Cost ($)
				Physical Characteristics				
24								
25								
26								
27								

NEW LICENSING OUT

	Project Name (P....)	To Firm (N°)	Minimum Annual Fee ($'000)
29			
30			
31			
32			
33			

NEW LICENSING IN

	Project Name (P....)	From Firm (N°)	Minimum Annual Fee ($'000)
34			
35			

MARKET RESEARCH STUDIES (Codes)

1	2	3	4	5	6	7	8	9	10	11	12	13	14	15	16
28															

ADMINISTRATIVE ADJUSTMENTS ($'000)

36		
	EC (—) EP (+)	BD (—) BI (+)

MODIFICATIONS RESULTING FROM NEGOTIATIONS BETWEEN
THE FIRM AND THE GAME ADMINISTRATOR

Source of Modification	Exceptional Profits (+) or Costs (—) ($'000)	Budget Increase (+) or Decrease (—) ($'000)
1. Additional information bought from the game administrator		
_____	_____	_____
_____	_____	_____
_____	_____	_____
_____	_____	_____
_____	_____	_____
_____	_____	_____
2. Payment to the Production Department by INDUSTRAT administration for liquidation of obsolete inventory		
Brand x Quantity ('000) x Manufacturing Cost x Proportion (%)		
_____ x _____ x _____ x _____	_____	
_____ x _____ x _____ x _____	_____	
_____ x _____ x _____ x _____	_____	
3. Changes in Marketing Expenditure Budget	_____	_____
	_____	_____
	_____	_____
	_____	_____
	_____	_____
	_____	_____
4. Fines		
_____	_____	_____
_____	_____	_____
_____	_____	_____
_____	_____	_____
5. Other Modifications		
_____	_____	_____
_____	_____	_____
_____	_____	_____
_____	_____	_____
TOTAL		

Signature of the firm's representative _____

Signature of the game administrator _____

INDUSTRAT DECISION FORM

Firm : _____   Industry : _____

Number of products for sale : _____   Period : _____

Number of development projects : _____

Number of new projects licensed out : _____

Number of new projects licensed in : _____

PRODUCT MANAGEMENT

	Product Name	Development Project (New/Mod Product Only)	Production ('000s)	List Price ($)	Maximum Price Discount (%)	Sales Force Commission (%)	Promotion ($' 000)	Product Advertising ($'000)	Allocation of Technical Support (%)
2									
3									
4									
5									
6									
7									
8									
9									
10									
11									100 %

SALES FORCE MANAGEMENT

12 Organizational Structure (code) ☐   Total Number of Salespersons ☐   Sales Force Training ($'000) ☐

ALLOCATION (%)

13 Geography

E	C	W
			100 %

14 Size

S	M	L
			100 %

15 End Product

I	CN	CR
			100 %

16 DMU

P	E	PU	G
				100 %

TECHNICAL FORCE MANAGEMENT

17 Total Number of Technicians ☐   Tech. Force Training ($'000) ☐

ALLOCATION (%)

18 Geography

E	C	W
			100 %

19 Size

S	M	L
			100 %

20 End Product

I	CN	CR
			100 %

21 DMU

P	E	PU	G
				100 %

CORPORATE MARKETING

22 Corporate Communications ($'000) ☐

RESEARCH AND DEVELOPMENT

Research

	Technology (Code)	Investment ($'000)
23		

Development

	Project Name (P. . .)	Technology (Code)	Budget ($'000)	1	2 Physical Characteristics 3	4	Base Cost ($)
24							
25							
26							
27							

NEW LICENSING OUT

	Project Name (P. . .)	To Firm (Nº)	Minimum Annual Fee ($'000)
29			
30			
31			
32			
33			

NEW LICENSING IN

	Project Name (P. . .)	From Firm (Nº)	Minimum Annual Fee ($'000)
34			
35			

MARKET RESEARCH STUDIES (Codes)

1	2	3	4	5	6	7	8	9	10	11	12	13	14	15	16
28 | | | | | | | | | | | | | | | | |

ADMINISTRATIVE ADJUSTMENTS ($'000)

36 | ☐ ☐

EC (—) EP (+)   BD (—) BI (+)

MODIFICATIONS RESULTING FROM NEGOTIATIONS BETWEEN
THE FIRM AND THE GAME ADMINISTRATOR

Source of Modification	Exceptional Profits (+) or Costs (—) ($'000)	Budget Increase (+) or Decrease (—) ($'000)
1. Additional information bought from the game administrator		
2. Payment to the Production Department by INDUSTRAT administration for liquidation of obsolete inventory		
3. Changes in Marketing Expenditure Budget		
4. Fines		
5. Other Modifications		
TOTAL		

Section 2 detail:

Brand   x   Quantity ('000)   x   Manufac- turing Cost   x   Proportion (%)

_____ x _____ x _____ x _____

_____ x _____ x _____ x _____

_____ x _____ x _____ x _____

Signature of the firm's representative _____

Signature of the game administrator _____

INDUSTRAT DECISION FORM

Firm _____

Number of products for sale _____

Number of development projects _____

Number of new projects licensed out _____

Number of new projects licensed in _____

Industry _____

Period _____

PRODUCT MANAGEMENT

	Product Name	Development Project (New/Mod Product Only)	Production ('000s)	List Price ($)	Maximum Price Discount (%)	Sales Force Commission (%)	Promotion ($'000)	Product Advertising ($'000)	Allocation of Technical Support (%)
2									
3									
4									
5									
6									
7									
8									
9									
10									
11									100 %

SALES FORCE MANAGEMENT

12 Organizational Structure (code) [ ]   Total Number of Salespersons [ ]   Sales Force Training ($'000) [ ]

ALLOCATION (%)

13 Geography

E	C	W	
			100 %
S	M	L	
			100 %
I	CN	CR	
			100 %
P	E	PU	G
			100 %

14 Size

15 End Product

16 DMU

TECHNICAL FORCE MANAGEMENT

17 Total Number of Technicians [ ]   Tech. Force Training ($'000) [ ]

ALLOCATION (%)

18 Geography

E	C	W	
			100 %
S	M	L	
			100 %
I	CN	CR	
			100 %
P	E	PU	G
			100 %

19 Size

20 End Product

21 DMU

CORPORATE MARKETING

22 Corporate Communications ($'000) [ ]

RESEARCH AND DEVELOPMENT

Research

Technology (Code)	Investment ($'000)
23 [ ]	[ ]

Development

	Project Name (P)	Technology (Code)	Budget ($'000)	Physical Characteristics 1	2	3	4	Base Cost ($)
24								
25								
26								
27								

NEW LICENSING OUT

	Project Name (P)	To Firm (N°)	Minimum Annual Fee ($'000)
29			
30			
31			
32			
33			

NEW LICENSING IN

	Project Name (P)	From Firm (N°)	Minimum Annual Fee ($'000)
34			
35			

MARKET RESEARCH STUDIES (Codes)

1	2	3	4	5	6	7	8	9	10	11	12	13	14	15	16
28															

ADMINISTRATIVE ADJUSTMENTS ($'000)

36	EC (—) EP (+)	BD (—) BI (+)

MODIFICATIONS RESULTING FROM NEGOTIATIONS BETWEEN
THE FIRM AND THE GAME ADMINISTRATOR

Source of Modification	Exceptional Profits (+) or Costs (—) ($'000)	Budget Increase (+) or Decrease (—) ($'000)
1. Additional information bought from the game administrator		
2. Payment to the Production Department by INDUSTRAT administration for liquidation of obsolete inventory		

		Quantity ('000)		Manufac- turing Cost		Proportion (%)		
Brand	x		x		x			
_____	x	_____	x	_____	x	_____		
_____	x	_____	x	_____	x	_____		
_____	x	_____	x	_____	x	_____		

Source of Modification	Exceptional Profits (+) or Costs (—) ($'000)	Budget Increase (+) or Decrease (—) ($'000)
3. Changes in Marketing Expenditure Budget		
4. Fines		
5. Other Modifications		
TOTAL		

Signature of the firm's representative _____

Signature of the game administrator _____

INDUSTRAT DECISION FORM

Firm : _____   Industry : _____

Number of products for sale : _____   Period : _____

Number of development projects : _____

Number of new projects licensed out : _____

Number of new projects licensed in : _____

PRODUCT MANAGEMENT

Product Name	Development Project (New/Mod Product Only)	Production ('000s)	List Price ($)	Maximum Price Discount (%)	Sales Force Commission (%)	Promotion ($' 000)	Product Advertising ($'000)	Allocation of Technical Support (%)
2								
3								
4								
5								
6								
7								
8								
9								
10								
11								100 %

SALES FORCE MANAGEMENT

12 Organizational Structure (code) [ ]   Total Number of Salespersons [ ]   Sales Force Training ($'000) [ ]

ALLOCATION (%)

13 Geography

E	C	W	100 %
S	M	L	100 %

14 Size

15 End Product

I	CN	CR	100 %
P	E	PU	G	100 %

16 DMU

TECHNICAL FORCE MANAGEMENT

17 Total Number of Technicians [ ]   Tech. Force Training ($'000) [ ]

ALLOCATION (%)

18 Geography

E	C	W	100 %
S	M	L	100 %

19 Size

20 End Product

I	CN	CR	100 %
P	E	PU	G	100 %

21 DMU

CORPORATE MARKETING

22 Corporate Communications ($'000) [ ]

RESEARCH AND DEVELOPMENT

Research

Technology (Code)   Investment ($'000)

23 [ ]   [ ]

Development

Project Name (P . . .)	Technology (Code)	Budget ($'000)	1	Physical Characteristics 2	3	4	Base Cost ($)
24							
25							
26							
27							

NEW LICENSING OUT

Project Name (P . . .)	To Firm (N°)	Minimum Annual Fee ($'000)
29		
30		
31		
32		
33		

NEW LICENSING IN

Project Name (P . . .)	From Firm (N°)	Minimum Annual Fee ($'000)
34		
35		

MARKET RESEARCH STUDIES (Codes)

1	2	3	4	5	6	7	8	9	10	11	12	13	14	15	16

ADMINISTRATIVE ADJUSTMENTS ($'000)

36 [ ] [ ]

EC (—) EP (+)   BD (—) BI (+)

MODIFICATIONS RESULTING FROM NEGOTIATIONS BETWEEN
THE FIRM AND THE GAME ADMINISTRATOR

Source of Modification	Exceptional Profits (+) or Costs (−) ($'000)	Budget Increase (+) or Decrease (−) ($'000)
1. Additional information bought from the game administrator		
2. Payment to the Production Department by INDUSTRAT administration for liquidation of obsolete inventory		
3. Changes in Marketing Expenditure Budget		
4. Fines		
5. Other Modifications		
TOTAL		

Section 2 layout:

Brand   x   Quantity ('000)   x   Manufac- turing Cost   x   Proportion (%)

_____ x _____ x _____ x _____

_____ x _____ x _____ x _____

_____ x _____ x _____ x _____

Signature of the firm's representative _____

Signature of the game administrator _____

INDUSTRAT DECISION FORM

Firm _____   Industry _____

Number of products for sale _____   Period _____

Number of development projects _____

Number of new projects licensed out _____

Number of new projects licensed in : _____

PRODUCT MANAGEMENT

	Product Name	Development Project (New/Mod Product Only)	Production ('000s)	List Price ($)	Maximum Price Discount (%)	Sales Force Commission (%)	Promotion ($ 000)	Product Advertising ($'000)	Allocation of Technical Support (%)
2									
3									
4									
5									
6									
7									
8									
9									
10									
11									
									100 %

SALES FORCE MANAGEMENT

12 Organizational Structure (code) [ ]   Total Number of Salespersons [ ]   Sales Force Training ($'000) [ ]

ALLOCATION (%)

13 Geography

E	C	W	100 %
S	M	L	100 %
I	CN	CR	100 %
P	E	PU	G	100 %

14 Size
15 End Product
16 DMU

TECHNICAL FORCE MANAGEMENT

17 Total Number of Technicians [ ]   Tech. Force Training ($'000) [ ]

ALLOCATION (%)

18 Geography

E	C	W	100 %
S	M	L	100 %
I	CN	CR	100 %
P	E	PU	G	100 %

19 Size
20 End Product
21 DMU

CORPORATE MARKETING

22 Corporate Communications ($'000) [ ]

RESEARCH AND DEVELOPMENT

Research

	Technology (Code)	Investment ($'000)
23		

Development

	Project Name (P....)	Technology (Code)	Budget ($'000)	Physical Characteristics 1	2	3	4	Base Cost ($)
24								
25								
26								
27								

NEW LICENSING OUT

	Project Name (P ...)	To Firm (N°)	Minimum Annual Fee ($'000)
29			
30			
31			
32			
33			

NEW LICENSING IN

	Project Name (P ...)	From Firm (N°)	Minimum Annual Fee ($'000)
34			
35			

MARKET RESEARCH STUDIES (Codes)

	1	2	3	4	5	6	7	8	9	10	11	12	13	14	15	16
28																

ADMINISTRATIVE ADJUSTMENTS ($'000)

36		

EC (—) EP (+)   BD (—) BI (+)

MODIFICATIONS RESULTING FROM NEGOTIATIONS BETWEEN
THE FIRM AND THE GAME ADMINISTRATOR

Source of Modification	Exceptional Profits (+) or Costs (—) ($'000)	Budget Increase (+) or Decrease (—) ($'000)
1. Additional information bought from the game administrator		
2. Payment to the Production Department by INDUSTRAT administration for liquidation of obsolete inventory		
3. Changes in Marketing Expenditure Budget		
4. Fines		
5. Other Modifications		
TOTAL		

For section 2:

Brand x   Quantity ('000) x   Manufac-turing Cost x   Proportion (%)

_____ x _____ x _____ x _____

_____ x _____ x _____ x _____

_____ x _____ x _____ x _____

Signature of the firm's representative _____

Signature of the game administrator _____

INDUSTRAT DECISION FORM

Firm : _____

Number of products for sale : _____

Number of development projects : _____

Number of new projects licensed out : _____

Number of new projects licensed in : _____

Industry : _____

Period : _____

PRODUCT MANAGEMENT

	Product Name	Development Project (New/Mod Product Only)	Production ('000s)	List Price ($)	Maximum Price Discount (%)	Sales Force Commission (%)	Promotion ($' 000)	Product Advertising ($'000)	Allocation of Technical Support (%)
2									
3									
4									
5									
6									
7									
8									
9									
10									
11									100 %

SALES FORCE MANAGEMENT

12 Organizational Structure (code) [ ]   Total Number of Salespersons [ ]   Sales Force Training ($'000) [ ]

ALLOCATION (%)

	E	C	W	
13 Geography				100 %

	S	M	L	
14 Size				100 %

	I	CN	CR	
15 End Product				100 %

	P	E	PU	G
16 DMU					100 %

TECHNICAL FORCE MANAGEMENT

17 Total Number of Technicians [ ]   Tech. Force Training ($'000) [ ]

ALLOCATION (%)

	E	C	W	
18 Geography				100 %

	S	M	L	
19 Size				100 %

	I	CN	CR	
20 End Product				100 %

	P	E	PU	G
21 DMU					100 %

CORPORATE MARKETING

22 Corporate Communications ($'000) [ ]

RESEARCH AND DEVELOPMENT

Research

	Technology (Code)	Investment ($'000)
23	[ ]	[ ]

Development

	Project Name (P . . .)	Technology (Code)	Budget ($'000)	1	2	3	4	Base Cost ($)
24								
25								
26								
27								

Physical Characteristics: columns 1, 2, 3, 4

NEW LICENSING OUT

	Project Name (P . . .)	To Firm (N°)	Minimum Annual Fee ($'000)
29			
30			
31			
32			
33			

NEW LICENSING IN

	Project Name (P . . .)	From Firm (N°)	Minimum Annual Fee ($'000)
34			
35			

MARKET RESEARCH STUDIES (Codes)

1	2	3	4	5	6	7	8	9	10	11	12	13	14	15	16
28															

ADMINISTRATIVE ADJUSTMENTS ($'000)

36		
	EC (—) EP (+)	BD (—) BI (+)

MODIFICATIONS RESULTING FROM NEGOTIATIONS BETWEEN
THE FIRM AND THE GAME ADMINISTRATOR

Source of Modification	Exceptional Profits (+) or Costs (—) ($'000)	Budget Increase (+) or Decrease (—) ($'000)
1. Additional information bought from the game administrator		
2. Payment to the Production Department by INDUSTRAT administration for liquidation of obsolete inventory		
3. Changes in Marketing Expenditure Budget		
4. Fines		
5. Other Modifications		
TOTAL		

For section 2:

Brand x Quantity ('000) x Manufac-turing Cost x Proportion (%)

Signature of the firm's representative _____

Signature of the game administrator _____

INDUSTRAT DECISION FORM

Firm : _____   Industry : _____

Number of products for sale : _____   Period : _____

Number of development projects : _____

Number of new projects licensed out : _____

Number of new projects licensed in : _____

PRODUCT MANAGEMENT

	Product Name	Development Project (New/Mod Product Only)	Production ('000s)	List Price ($)	Maximum Price Discount (%)	Sales Force Commission (%)	Promotion ($ 000)	Product Advertising ($'000)	Allocation of Technical Support (%)
2									
3									
4									
5									
6									
7									
8									
9									
10									
11									100 %

SALES FORCE MANAGEMENT

12 Organizational Structure (code) [ ]   Total Number of Salespersons [ ]   Sales Force Training ($'000) [ ]

ALLOCATION (%)

13 Geography

14 Size

15 End Product

16 DMU

E	C	W	100 %
S	M	L	100 %
I	CN	CR	100 %
P	E	PU	G	100 %

TECHNICAL FORCE MANAGEMENT

17 Total Number of Technicians [ ]   Tech. Force Training ($'000) [ ]

ALLOCATION (%)

18 Geography

19 Size

20 End Product

21 DMU

E	C	W	100 %
S	M	L	100 %
I	CN	CR	100 %
P	E	PU	G	100 %

CORPORATE MARKETING

22 Corporate Communications ($'000) [ ]

RESEARCH AND DEVELOPMENT

Research

	Technology (Code)	Investment ($'000)
23		

Development

	Project Name (P . . . .)	Technology (Code)	Budget ($'000)	Physical Characteristics 1	2	3	4	Base Cost ($)
24								
25								
26								
27								

NEW LICENSING OUT

	Project Name (P . . .)	To Firm (N°)	Minimum Annual Fee ($'000)
29			
30			
31			
32			
33			

NEW LICENSING IN

	Project Name (P . . .)	From Firm (N°)	Minimum Annual Fee ($'000)
34			
35			

MARKET RESEARCH STUDIES (Codes)

1	2	3	4	5	6	7	8	9	10	11	12	13	14	15	16
28															

ADMINISTRATIVE ADJUSTMENTS ($'000)

36		
	EC (—) EP (+)	BD (—) BI (+)

MODIFICATIONS RESULTING FROM NEGOTIATIONS BETWEEN
THE FIRM AND THE GAME ADMINISTRATOR

Source of Modification	Exceptional Profits (+) or Costs (—) ($'000)	Budget Increase (+) or Decrease (—) ($'000)
1. Additional information bought from the game administrator		
2. Payment to the Production Department by INDUSTRAT administration for liquidation of obsolete inventory		
3. Changes in Marketing Expenditure Budget		
4. Fines		
5. Other Modifications		
TOTAL		

2. Payment to the Production Department by INDUSTRAT administration for liquidation of obsolete inventory

Brand x Quantity ('000) x Manufacturing Cost x Proportion (%)

_____ x _____ x _____ x _____

_____ x _____ x _____ x _____

_____ x _____ x _____ x _____

Signature of the firm's representative _____

Signature of the game administrator _____

INDUSTRAT DECISION FORM

Firm : _____   Industry : _____

Number of products for sale : _____   Period : _____

Number of development projects : _____

Number of new projects licensed out : _____

Number of new projects licensed in : _____

PRODUCT MANAGEMENT

	Product Name	Development Project (New/Mod Product Only)	Production ('000s)	List Price ($)	Maximum Price Discount (%)	Sales Force Commission (%)	Promotion ($'000)	Product Advertising ($'000)	Allocation of Technical Support (%)
2									
3									
4									
5									
6									
7									
8									
9									
10									
11									
									100 %

SALES FORCE MANAGEMENT

12 Organizational Structure (code) [ ]   Total Number of Salespersons [ ]   Sales Force Training ($'000) [ ]

ALLOCATION (%)

13 Geography

E	C	W	100 %

14 Size

S	M	L	100 %

15 End Product

I	CN	CR	100 %

16 DMU

P	E	PU	G	100 %

TECHNICAL FORCE MANAGEMENT

17 Total Number of Technicians [ ]   Tech Force Training ($'000) [ ]

ALLOCATION (%)

18 Geography

E	C	W	100 %

19 Size

S	M	L	100 %

20 End Product

I	CN	CR	100 %

21 DMU

P	E	PU	G	100 %

CORPORATE MARKETING

22 Corporate Communications ($'000) [ ]

RESEARCH AND DEVELOPMENT

Research

Technology (Code)	Investment ($'000)
23 [ ]	[ ]

Development

	Project Name (P . . .)	Technology (Code)	Budget ($'000)	1	Physical Characteristics 2	3	4	Base Cost ($)
24								
25								
26								
27								

NEW LICENSING OUT

	Project Name (P . . .)	To Firm (Nº)	Minimum Annual Fee ($'000)
29			
30			
31			
32			
33			

NEW LICENSING IN

	Project Name (P . . .)	From Firm (Nº)	Minimum Annual Fee ($'000)
34			
35			

MARKET RESEARCH STUDIES (Codes)

1	2	3	4	5	6	7	8	9	10	11	12	13	14	15	16
28															

ADMINISTRATIVE ADJUSTMENTS ($'000)

36 [   ]

EC (—) EP (+)   BD (—) BI (+)

MODIFICATIONS RESULTING FROM NEGOTIATIONS BETWEEN
THE FIRM AND THE GAME ADMINISTRATOR

Source of Modification	Exceptional Profits (+) or Costs (—) ($'000)	Budget Increase (+) or Decrease (—) ($'000)
1. Additional information bought from the game administrator		
2. Payment to the Production Department by INDUSTRAT administration for liquidation of obsolete inventory		
3. Changes in Marketing Expenditure Budget		
4. Fines		
5. Other Modifications		
TOTAL		

For section 2:

Brand x Quantity ('000) x Manufac-turing Cost x Proportion (%)

_____ x _____ x _____ x _____
_____ x _____ x _____ x _____
_____ x _____ x _____ x _____

Signature of the firm's representative _____

Signature of the game administrator _____

INDUSTRAT DECISION FORM

Firm : _____

Number of products for sale : _____

Number of development projects : _____

Number of new projects licensed out : _____

Number of new projects licensed in : _____

Industry : _____

Period : _____

PRODUCT MANAGEMENT

	Product Name	Development Project (New/Mod Product Only)	Production ('000s)	List Price ($)	Maximum Price Discount (%)	Sales Force Commission (%)	Promotion ($ 000)	Product Advertising ($'000)	Allocation of Technical Support (%)
2									
3									
4									
5									
6									
7									
8									
9									
10									
11									100 %

SALES FORCE MANAGEMENT

12 Organizational Structure (code) [ ]   Total Number of Salespersons [ ]   Sales Force Training ($'000) [ ]

ALLOCATION (%)

13 Geography

14 Size

15 End Product

16 DMU

E	C	W	100 %
S	M	L	100 %
I	CN	CR	100 %
P	E	PU	G	100 %

TECHNICAL FORCE MANAGEMENT

17 Total Number of Technicians [ ]   Tech. Force Training ($'000) [ ]

ALLOCATION (%)

18 Geography

19 Size

20 End Product

21 DMU

E	C	W	100 %
S	M	L	100 %
I	CN	CR	100 %
P	E	PU	G	100 %

CORPORATE MARKETING

22 Corporate Communications ($'000) [ ]

RESEARCH AND DEVELOPMENT

Research

Technology (Code)   Investment ($'000)

23 [ ] [ ]

Development

	Project Name (P...)	Technology (Code)	Budget ($'000)	Physical Characteristics 1	2	3	4	Base Cost ($)
24								
25								
26								
27								

NEW LICENSING OUT

	Project Name (P...)	To Firm (Nº)	Minimum Annual Fee ($'000)
29			
30			
31			
32			
33			

NEW LICENSING IN

	Project Name (P...)	From Firm (Nº)	Minimum Annual Fee ($'000)
34			
35			

MARKET RESEARCH STUDIES (Codes)

1	2	3	4	5	6	7	8	9	10	11	12	13	14	15	16

28

ADMINISTRATIVE ADJUSTMENTS ($'000)

36 [ ]

EC (—) EP (+)   BD (—) BI (+)

MODIFICATIONS RESULTING FROM NEGOTIATIONS BETWEEN
THE FIRM AND THE GAME ADMINISTRATOR

Source of Modification	Exceptional Profits (+) or Costs (—) ($'000)	Budget Increase (+) or Decrease (—) ($'000)
1. Additional information bought from the game administrator		
2. Payment to the Production Department by INDUSTRAT administration for liquidation of obsolete inventory		
3. Changes in Marketing Expenditure Budget		
4. Fines		
5. Other Modifications		
TOTAL		

2. Payment to the Production Department by INDUSTRAT administration for liquidation of obsolete inventory

Brand   x   Quantity ('000)   x   Manufac- turing Cost   x   Proportion (%)

_____ x _____ x _____ x _____

_____ x _____ x _____ x _____

_____ x _____ x _____ x _____

Signature of the firm's representative _____

Signature of the game administrator _____

INDUSTRAT BUDGETING FORM

Industry _____

Firm _____

Period _____

												TOTALS	
Product Name														
Production ('000 Units)														
Quantity Sold ('000 Units)														
Inventory ('000 Units)														
List Price ($)														
Average Price ($)														
Unit Manufacturing Costs ($)														
Unit Licensing Costs ($)														
Unit Commissions ($)														
Total Unit Costs														
Revenue from Sales ($'000)														
Manufacturing Costs ($'000)														
Licensing Costs ($'000)														
Sales Commission ($'000)														
Promotion ($'000)														Prom.
Product Advertising ($'000)														Pr Adv.
Technical Support * ($'000)														Tech.
Inventory Holding Costs ($'000)														
Gross Marketing Contribution ($'000)													TOTAL	

Fixed Sales Force Costs ($'000) ....

Sales Force Training Costs ($'000) ....

Corporate Communication ($'000) ....

Research ($'000) ....

Development ($'000) ....

Market Research ($'000) ....

Total Marketing Expenditures ....

Operational Marketing Contribution ($'000) ....

Revenue from Licensing ($'000) ....

Exceptional Costs or Profits ($'000) ....

Net Marketing Contribution ($'000) ....

* (Total package of technical support) x (proportion allocated to the individual product, as per decision form).

SALES FORECAST INPUT FOR BUDGETING

PRODUCT	AGGREGATE	MACROSEGMENTATION SCHEME CHOSEN *									UNIT SALES
		REGIONS			ACCOUNT POTENTIAL			END USE			
		EAST	CENTRAL	WEST	SMALL	MEDIUM	LARGE	COMM.	INST.	CONS.	
KOREX MARKET FORECAST ('000 UNITS)											
LOMEX MARKET FORECAST ** ('000 UNITS)											

1											
2											
3											
4											
5											
6											
7											
8											
9											
10											

* Please use only the columns applicable to the macrosegmentation scheme (s) you choose.

** You may apply your expected shares in segment/market to compute your corresponding sales forecasts.

INDUSTRAT BUDGETING FORM

Industry_____

Firm _____

Period _____

Product Name											
Production ('000 Units)											
Quantity Sold ('000 Units)											
Inventory ('000 Units)											
List Price ($)											
Average Price ($)											
Unit Manufacturing Costs ($)											
Unit Licensing Costs ($)											
Unit Commissions ($)											
Total Unit Costs											
Revenue from Sales ($'000)											
Manufacturing Costs ($'000)											
Licensing Costs ($'000)											
Sales Commission ($'000)											
Promotion ($'000)											TOTALS
Product Advertising ($'000)											Prom.
Technical Support * ($'000)											Pr Adv
Inventory Holding Costs ($'000)											Tech.
Gross Marketing Contribution ($'000)											TOTAL

Fixed Sales Force Costs ($'000)	
Sales Force Training Costs ($'000)	
Corporate Communication ($'000)	
Research ($'000)	
Development ($'000)	
Market Research ($'000)	
Total Marketing Expenditures	
Operational Marketing Contribution ($'000)	
Revenue from Licensing ($'000)	
Exceptional Costs or Profits ($'000)	
Net Marketing Contribution ($'000)	

* (Total package of technical support) x (proportion allocated to the individual product, as per decision form)

SALES FORECAST INPUT FOR BUDGETING

PRODUCT	AGGREGATE	MACROSEGMENTATION SCHEME CHOSEN *									UNIT SALES
		REGIONS			ACCOUNT POTENTIAL			END USE			
		EAST	CENTRAL	WEST	SMALL	MEDIUM	LARGE	COMM.	INST.	CONS.	
KOREX MARKET FORECAST (000 UNITS)											
LOMEX MARKET FORECAST ** (000 UNITS)											

1											
2											
3											
4											
5											
6											
7											
8											
9											
10											

* Please use only the columns applicable to the macrosegmentation scheme (s) you choose.

** You may apply your expected shares in segment/market to compute your corresponding sales forecasts.

INDUSTRAT BUDGETING FORM

Industry _____

Firm _____

Period _____

Product Name											
Production ('000 Units)											
Quantity Sold ('000 Units)											
Inventory ('000 Units)											
List Price ($)											
Average Price ($)											
Unit Manufacturing Costs ($)											
Unit Licensing Costs ($)											
Unit Commissions ($)											
Total Unit Costs											
Revenue from Sales ($'000)											
Manufacturing Costs ($'000)											
Licensing Costs ($'000)											
Sales Commission ($'000)											
Promotion ($'000)												TOTALS
Product Advertising ($'000)												Prom.
Technical Support * ($'000)												Pr Adv.
Inventory Holding Costs ($'000)												Tech.
Gross Marketing Contribution ($'000)												TOTAL

Fixed Sales Force Costs ($'000) ....

Sales Force Training Costs ($'000) ....

Corporate Communication ($'000) ....

Research ($'000) ....

Development ($'000) ....

Market Research ($'000) ....

Total Marketing Expenditures ....

Operational Marketing Contribution ($'000) ....

Revenue from Licensing ($'000) ....

Exceptional Costs or Profits ($'000) ....

Net Marketing Contribution ($'000) ....

* (Total package of technical support) x (proportion allocated to the individual product, as per decision form).

SALES FORECAST INPUT FOR BUDGETING

PRODUCT	AGGREGATE	MACROSEGMENTATION SCHEME CHOSEN *									UNIT SALES
		REGIONS			ACCOUNT POTENTIAL			END USE			
		EAST	CENTRAL	WEST	SMALL	MEDIUM	LARGE	COMM.	INST.	CONS.	
KOREX MARKET FORECAST ('000 UNITS)											
LOMEX MARKET FORECAST ** ('000 UNITS)											

1											
2											
3											
4											
5											
6											
7											
8											
9											
10											

* Please use only the columns applicable to the macrosegmentation scheme (s) you choose.

** You may apply your expected shares in segment/market to compute your corresponding sales forecasts.

INDUSTRAT BUDGETING FORM

Industry _____

Firm _____

Period _____

											TOTALS	
Product Name												
Production ('000 Units)												
Quantity Sold ('000 Units)												
Inventory ('000 Units)												
List Price ($)												
Average Price ($)												
Unit Manufacturing Costs ($)												
Unit Licensing Costs ($)												
Unit Commissions ($)												
Total Unit Costs												
Revenue from Sales ($'000)												
Manufacturing Costs ($'000)												
Licensing Costs ($'000)												
Sales Commission ($'000)												
Promotion ($'000)													Prom.
Product Advertising ($'000)													Pr Adv
Technical Support * ($'000)													Tech.
Inventory Holding Costs ($'000)												
											TOTAL	
Gross Marketing Contribution ($'000)												

Fixed Sales Force Costs ($'000)	
Sales Force Training Costs ($'000)	
Corporate Communication ($'000)	
Research ($'000)	
Development ($'000)	
Market Research ($'000)	
Total Marketing Expenditures	
Operational Marketing Contribution ($'000)	
Revenue from Licensing ($'000)	
Exceptional Costs or Profits ($'000)	
Net Marketing Contribution ($'000)	

* (Total package of technical support) x (proportion allocated to the individual prod.. as per decision form).

SALES FORECAST INPUT FOR BUDGETING

| PRODUCT | AGGREGATE | MACROSEGMENTATION SCHEME CHOSEN * | | | | | | | | | UNIT SALES |
| | | REGIONS | | | ACCOUNT POTENTIAL | | | END USE | | | |
		EAST	CENTRAL	WEST	SMALL	MEDIUM	LARGE	COMM.	INST.	CONS.	
KOREX MARKET FORECAST (000 UNITS)											
LOMEX MARKET FORECAST ** (000 UNITS)											
1											
2											
3											
4											
5											
6											
7											
8											
9											
10											

* Please use only the columns applicable to the macrosegmentation scheme (s you choose.

** You may apply your expected shares in segment/market to compute your corresponding sales forecasts.

INDUSTRAT BUDGETING FORM

Industry _____
Firm _____
Period _____

												TOTALS	
Product Name													
Production ('000 Units)													
Quantity Sold ('000 Units)													
Inventory ('000 Units)													
List Price ($)													
Average Price ($)													
Unit Manufacturing Costs ($)													
Unit Licensing Costs ($)													
Unit Commissions ($)													
Total Unit Costs													
Revenue from Sales ($'000)													
Manufacturing Costs ($'000)													
Licensing Costs ($'000)													
Sales Commission ($'000)													
Promotion ($'000)													Prom.
Product Advertising ($'000)													Pr Adv.
Technical Support * ($'000)													Tech.
Inventory Holding Costs ($'000)													
Gross Marketing Contribution ($'000)													TOTAL

Fixed Sales Force Costs ($'000)	
Sales Force Training Costs ($'000)	
Corporate Communication ($'000)	
Research ($'000)	
Development ($'000)	
Market Research ($'000)	
Total Marketing Expenditures	
Operational Marketing Contribution ($'000)	
Revenue from Licensing ($'000)	
Exceptional Costs or Profits ($'000)	
Net Marketing Contribution ($'000)	

* (Total package of technical support) x (proportion allocated to the individual product, as per decision form).

SALES FORECAST INPUT FOR BUDGETING

PRODUCT	AGGREGATE	MACROSEGMENTATION SCHEME CHOSEN *									UNIT SALES
		REGIONS			ACCOUNT POTENTIAL			END USE			
		EAST	CENTRAL	WEST	SMALL	MEDIUM	LARGE	COMM.	INST.	CONS.	
KOREX MARKET FORECAST (000 UNITS)											
LOMEX MARKET FORECAST * * (000 UNITS)											

1											
2											
3											
4											
5											
6											
7											
8											
9											
10											

* Please use only the columns applicable to the macrosegmentation scheme (s) you choose.

* * You may apply your expected shares in segment/market to compute your corresponding sales forecasts.

INDUSTRAT BUDGETING FORM

Industry _____

Firm _____

Period _____

											TOTALS	
Product Name												
Production ('000 Units)												
Quantity Sold ('000 Units)												
Inventory ('000 Units)												
List Price ($)												
Average Price ($)												
Unit Manufacturing Costs ($)												
Unit Licensing Costs ($)												
Unit Commissions ($)												
Total Unit Costs												
Revenue from Sales ($'000)												
Manufacturing Costs ($'000)												
Licensing Costs ($'000)												
Sales Commission ($'000)											TOTALS	
Promotion ($'000)												Prom.
Product Advertising ($'000)												Pr Adv.
Technical Support * ($'000)												Tech.
Inventory Holding Costs ($'000)												
Gross Marketing Contribution ($'000)											TOTAL	

Fixed Sales Force Costs ($'000)	
Sales Force Training Costs ($'000)	
Corporate Communication ($'000)	
Research ($'000)	
Development ($'000)	
Market Research ($'000)	
Total Marketing Expenditures	
Operational Marketing Contribution ($'000)	
Revenue from Licensing ($'000)	
Exceptional Costs or Profits ($'000)	
Net Marketing Contribution ($'000)	

* (Total package of technical support) x (proportion allocated to the individual product, as per decision form).

SALES FORECAST INPUT FOR BUDGETING

PRODUCT	AGGREGATE	MACROSEGMENTATION SCHEME CHOSEN *									UNIT SALES
		REGIONS			ACCOUNT POTENTIAL			END USE			
		EAST	CENTRAL	WEST	SMALL	MEDIUM	LARGE	COMM	INST	CONS.	
KOREX MARKET FORECAST (000 UNITS)											
LOMEX MARKET FORECAST * * (000 UNITS)											

1											
2											
3											
4											
5											
6											
7											
8											
9											
10											

* Please use only the columns applicable to the macrosegmentation scheme(s) you choose.

* * You may apply your expected shares in segment/market to compute your corresponding sales forecasts.

INDUSTRAT BUDGETING FORM

Industry _____

Firm _____

Period _____

												TOTALS	
Product Name													
Production ('000 Units)													
Quantity Sold ('000 Units)													
Inventory ('000 Units)													
List Price ($)													
Average Price ($)													
Unit Manufacturing Costs ($)													
Unit Licensing Costs ($)													
Unit Commissions ($)													
Total Unit Costs													
Revenue from Sales ($'000)													
Manufacturing Costs ($'000)													
Licensing Costs ($'000)													
Sales Commission ($'000)													
Promotion ($'000)													Prom.
Product Advertising ($'000)													Pr Adv.
Technical Support * ($'000)													Tech.
Inventory Holding Costs ($'000)													
Gross Marketing Contribution ($'000)												TOTAL	

	TOTAL
Fixed Sales Force Costs ($'000)	
Sales Force Training Costs ($'000)	
Corporate Communication ($'000)	
Research ($'000)	
Development ($'000)	
Market Research ($'000)	
Total Marketing Expenditures	
Operational Marketing Contribution ($'000)	
Revenue from Licensing ($'000)	
Exceptional Costs or Profits ($'000)	
Net Marketing Contribution ($'000)	

* (Total package of technical support) x (proportion allocated to the individual product, as per decision form).

SALES FORECAST INPUT FOR BUDGETING

PRODUCT	AGGREGATE	MACROSEGMENTATION SCHEME CHOSEN *									UNIT SALES
		REGIONS			ACCOUNT POTENTIAL			END USE			
		EAST	CENTRAL	WEST	SMALL	MEDIUM	LARGE	COMM.	INST.	CONS.	
KOREX MARKET FORECAST (000 UNITS)											
LOMEX MARKET FORECAST ** (000 UNITS)											

1											
2											
3											
4											
5											
6											
7											
8											
9											
10											

* Please use only the columns applicable to the macrosegmentation scheme (as you choose).

** You may apply your expected shares in segment/market to compute your corresponding sales forecasts.

INDUSTRAT BUDGETING FORM

Industry_____

Firm _____

Period _____

												TOTALS	
Product Name													
Production ('000 Units)													
Quantity Sold ('000 Units)													
Inventory ('000 Units)													
List Price ($)													
Average Price ($)													
Unit Manufacturing Costs ($)													
Unit Licensing Costs ($)													
Unit Commissions ($)													
Total Unit Costs													
Revenue from Sales ($'000)													
Manufacturing Costs ($'000)													
Licensing Costs ($'000)													
Sales Commission ($'000)													
Promotion ($'000)													Prom.
Product Advertising ($'000)													Pr Adv.
Technical Support * ($'000)													Tech.
Inventory Holding Costs ($'000)													
Gross Marketing Contribution ($'000)												TOTAL	

Fixed Sales Force Costs ($'000)	
Sales Force Training Costs ($'000)	
Corporate Communication ($'000)	
Research ($'000)	
Development ($'000)	
Market Research ($'000)	
Total Marketing Expenditures	
Operational Marketing Contribution ($'000)	
Revenue from Licensing ($'000)	
Exceptional Costs or Profits ($'000)	
Net Marketing Contribution ($'000)	

* (Total package of technical support) x (proportion allocated to the individual product, as per decision form).

SALES FORECAST INPUT FOR BUDGETING

PRODUCT	AGGREGATE	MACROSEGMENTATION SCHEME CHOSEN *									UNIT SALES
		REGIONS			ACCOUNT POTENTIAL			END USE			
		EAST	CENTRAL	WEST	SMALL	MEDIUM	LARGE	COMM.	INST.	CONS.	
KOREX MARKET FORECAST ('000 UNITS)											
LOMEX MARKET FORECAST * * ('000 UNITS)											

1											
2											
3											
4											
5											
6											
7											
8											
9											
10											

* Please use only the columns applicable to the macrosegmentation scheme (s) you choose.

* * You may apply your expected shares in segment/market to compute your corresponding sales forecasts.

INDUSTRAT BUDGETING FORM

Industry _____

Firm _____

Period _____

Product Name											
Production ('000 Units)											
Quantity Sold ('000 Units)											
Inventory ('000 Units)											
List Price ($)											
Average Price ($)											
Unit Manufacturing Costs ($)											
Unit Licensing Costs ($)											
Unit Commissions ($)											
Total Unit Costs											
Revenue from Sales ($'000)											
Manufacturing Costs ($'000)											
Licensing Costs ($'000)											
Sales Commission ($'000)											
Promotion ($'000)											
Product Advertising ($'000)											
Technical Support * ($'000)											
Inventory Holding Costs ($'000)											

TOTALS

Prom.

Pr Adv

Tech.

Gross Marketing Contribution ($'000)											TOTAL

Fixed Sales Force Costs ($'000) ....

Sales Force Training Costs ($'000) ....

Corporate Communication ($'000) ....

Research ($'000) ....

Development ($'000) ....

Market Research ($'000) ....

Total Marketing Expenditures ....

Operational Marketing Contribution ($'000) ....

Revenue from Licensing ($'000) ....

Exceptional Costs or Profits ($'000) ....

Net Marketing Contribution ($'000) ....

* (Total package of technical support) x (proportion allocated to the individual product, as per decision form).

SALES FORECAST INPUT FOR BUDGETING

PRODUCT	AGGREGATE	MACROSEGMENTATION SCHEME CHOSEN *									UNIT SALES
		REGIONS			ACCOUNT POTENTIAL			END USE			
		EAST	CENTRAL	WEST	SMALL	MEDIUM	LARGE	COMM.	INST.	CONS.	
KOREX MARKET FORECAST ('000 UNITS)											
LOMEX MARKET FORECAST ** ('000 UNITS)											

1											
2											
3											
4											
5											
6											
7											
8											
9											
10											

* Please use only the columns applicable to the macrosegmentation scheme(s) you choose.

** You may apply your expected shares in segment/market to compute your corresponding sales forecasts.

INDUSTRAT BUDGETING FORM

Industry _____

Firm _____

Period _____

Product Name											
Production ('000 Units)											
Quantity Sold ('000 Units)											
Inventory ('000 Units)											
List Price ($)											
Average Price ($)											
Unit Manufacturing Costs ($)											
Unit Licensing Costs ($)											
Unit Commissions ($)											
Total Unit Costs											
Revenue from Sales ($'000)											
Manufacturing Costs ($'000)											
Licensing Costs ($'000)											
Sales Commission ($'000)											
Promotion ($'000)											TOTALS
Product Advertising ($'000)											Prom.
Technical Support * ($'000)											Pr Adv.
Inventory Holding Costs ($'000)											Tech.
Gross Marketing Contribution ($'000)											TOTAL

Fixed Sales Force Costs ($'000)	
Sales Force Training Costs ($'000)	
Corporate Communication ($'000)	
Research ($'000)	
Development ($'000)	
Market Research ($'000)	
Total Marketing Expenditures	
Operational Marketing Contribution ($'000)	
Revenue from Licensing ($'000)	
Exceptional Costs or Profits ($'000)	
Net Marketing Contribution ($'000)	

* (Total package of technical support) x (proportion allocated to the individual product, as per decision form).

SALES FORECAST INPUT FOR BUDGETING

PRODUCT	AGGREGATE	MACROSEGMENTATION SCHEME CHOSEN *									UNIT SALES
		REGIONS			ACCOUNT POTENTIAL			END USE			
		EAST	CENTRAL	WEST	SMALL	MEDIUM	LARGE	COMM.	INST.	CONS.	
KOREX MARKET FORECAST ('000 UNITS)											
LOMEX MARKET FORECAST * * ('000 UNITS)											

1											
2											
3											
4											
5											
6											
7											
8											
9											
10											

* Please use only the columns applicable to the macrosegmentation scheme (s) you choose.

* * You may apply your expected shares in segment/market to compute your corresponding sales forecasts.

INDUSTRAT BUDGETING FORM

Industry_____

Firm _____

Period _____

Product Name												
Production ('000 Units)												
Quantity Sold ('000 Units)												
Inventory ('000 Units)												
List Price ($)												
Average Price ($)												
Unit Manufacturing Costs ($)												
Unit Licensing Costs ($)												
Unit Commissions ($)												
Total Unit Costs												
Revenue from Sales ($'000)												
Manufacturing Costs ($'000)												
Licensing Costs ($'000)												
Sales Commission ($'000)												
Promotion ($'000)												TOTALS
Product Advertising ($'000)												Prom.
Technical Support * ($'000)												Pr Adv
Inventory Holding Costs ($'000)												Tech.
Gross Marketing Contribution ($'000)												TOTAL

Fixed Sales Force Costs ($'000)	
Sales Force Training Costs ($'000)	
Corporate Communication ($'000)	
Research ($'000)	
Development ($'000)	
Market Research ($'000)	
Total Marketing Expenditures	
Operational Marketing Contribution ($'000)	
Revenue from Licensing ($'000)	
Exceptional Costs or Profits ($'000)	
Net Marketing Contribution ($'000)	

* (Total package of technical support) x (proportion allocated to the individual product, as per decision form)

SALES FORECAST INPUT FOR BUDGETING

PRODUCT	AGGREGATE	MACROSEGMENTATION SCHEME CHOSEN *									UNIT SALES
		REGIONS			ACCOUNT POTENTIAL			END USE			
		EAST	CENTRAL	WEST	SMALL	MEDIUM	LARGE	COMM.	INST.	CONS.	
KOREX MARKET FORECAST (000 UNITS)											
LOMEX MARKET FORECAST * * (000 UNITS)											

1											
2											
3											

4											
5											
6											

7											
8											
9											
10											

* Please use only the columns applicable to the macrosegmentation scheme (s) you choose.

* * You may apply your expected shares in segment/market to compute your corresponding sales forecasts.

INDUSTRAT BUDGETING FORM

Industry_____

Firm _____

Period _____

Product Name										
Production ('000 Units)										
Quantity Sold ('000 Units)										
Inventory ('000 Units)										
List Price ($)										
Average Price ($)										
Unit Manufacturing Costs ($)										
Unit Licensing Costs ($)										
Unit Commissions ($)										
Total Unit Costs										
Revenue from Sales ($'000)										
Manufacturing Costs ($'000)										
Licensing Costs ($'000)										
Sales Commission ($'000)										
Promotion ($'000)										
Product Advertising ($'000)										
Technical Support * ($'000)										
Inventory Holding Costs ($'000)										
Gross Marketing Contribution ($'000)										

TOTALS

Prom.

Pr Adv

Tech.

TOTAL

Fixed Sales Force Costs ($'000)..

Sales Force Training Costs ($'000)..

Corporate Communication ($'000)..

Research ($'000)..

Development ($'000)..

Market Research ($'000)..

Total Marketing Expenditures..

Operational Marketing Contribution ($'000)..

Revenue from Licensing ($'000)..

Exceptional Costs or Profits ($'000)..

Net Marketing Contribution ($'000)..

* (Total package of technical support) x (proportion allocated to the individual product, as per decision form).

SALES FORECAST INPUT FOR BUDGETING

| PRODUCT | AGGREGATE | MACROSEGMENTATION SCHEME CHOSEN * | | | | | | | | | UNIT SALES |
| | | REGIONS | | | ACCOUNT POTENTIAL | | | END USE | | | |
		EAST	CENTRAL	WEST	SMALL	MEDIUM	LARGE	COMM.	INST.	CONS.	
KOREX MARKET FORECAST ('000 UNITS)											
LOMEX MARKET FORECAST * * ('000 UNITS)											

1											
2											
3											

4											
5											
6											

7											
8											
9											
10											

*   Please use only the columns applicable to the macrosegmentation scheme (s) you choose.

* * You may apply your expected shares in segment/market to compute your corresponding sales forecasts.

INDUSTRAT STRATEGIC PLANNING FORM

_____

_____

_____

_____

_____

_____

_____

_____

_____

_____

_____

_____

_____

_____

_____

_____

_____

_____

_____

_____

_____

_____

_____

_____

FORECAST RESULTING FROM STRATEGIC PLANNING

Firm_____   Industry_____

GENERAL PERFORMANCE		1	2	3	4	5	6	7	8	9	10
Market Share (%) of $ Sales	Objective										
	Outcome										
Sales Revenue ($'000)	Objective										
	Outcome										
Manufacturing Costs ($'000)	Objective										
	Outcome										
Sales Commission ($'000)	Objective										
	Outcome										

PRODUCT MARKETING EXPENDITURES

		1	2	3	4	5	6	7	8	9	10
Promotion ($'000)	Objective										
	Outcome										
Product Advertising ($'000)	Objective										
	Outcome										
Technical Support ($'000)	Objective										
	Outcome										
Licensing Costs ($'000)	Objective										
	Outcome										

UNALLOCATED MARKETING EXPENDITURES

		1	2	3	4	5	6	7	8	9	10
Fixed Sales Force Costs ($'000)	Objective										
	Outcome										
Sales Force Training Costs ($'000)	Objective										
	Outcome										
Corporate Communication ($'000)	Objective										
	Outcome										
Research ($'000)	Objective										
	Outcome										
Development ($'000)	Objective										
	Outcome										
Market Research ($'000)	Objective										
	Outcome										
Total Marketing Expenditures ($'000)	Objective										
	Outcome										
Operational Contribution ($'000)	Objective										
	Outcome										
Licensing Revenues ($'000)	Objective										
	Outcome										

		1	2	3	4	5	6	7	8	9	10
Net Marketing Contribution ($'000)	Objective										
	Outcome										
Others ($'000)	Objective										
	Outcome										

INDUSTRAT STRATEGIC PLANNING FORM

_____

_____

_____

_____

_____

_____

_____

_____

_____

_____

_____

_____

_____

_____

_____

_____

_____

_____

_____

_____

_____

_____

_____

_____

_____

FORECAST RESULTING FROM STRATEGIC PLANNING

Firm_____   Industry_____

GENERAL PERFORMANCE		1	2	3	4	5	6	7	8	9	10
Market Share (%) of $ Sales	Objective										
	Outcome										
Sales Revenue ($'000)	Objective										
	Outcome										
Manufacturing Costs ($'000)	Objective										
	Outcome										
Sales Commission ($'000)	Objective										
	Outcome										

PRODUCT MARKETING EXPENDITURES

Promotion ($'000)	Objective										
	Outcome										
Product Advertising ($'000)	Objective										
	Outcome										
Technical Support ($'000)	Objective										
	Outcome										
Licensing Costs ($'000)	Objective										
	Outcome										

UNALLOCATED MARKETING EXPENDITURES

Fixed Sales Force Costs ($'000)	Objective										
	Outcome										
Sales Force Training Costs ($'000)	Objective										
	Outcome										
Corporate Communication ($'000)	Objective										
	Outcome										
Research ($'000)	Objective										
	Outcome										
Development ($'000)	Objective										
	Outcome										
Market Research ($'000)	Objective										
	Outcome										
Total Marketing Expenditures ($'000)	Objective										
	Outcome										
Operational Contribution ($'000)	Objective										
	Outcome										
Licensing Revenues ($'000)	Objective										
	Outcome										

Net Marketing Contribution ($'000)	Objective										
	Outcome										
Others ($'000)	Objective										
	Outcome										

INDUSTRAT STRATEGIC PLANNING FORM

FORECAST RESULTING FROM STRATEGIC PLANNING

Firm_____   Industry_____

GENERAL PERFORMANCE		1	2	3	4	5	6	7	8	9	10
Market Share (%) of $ Sales	Objective										
	Outcome										
Sales Revenue ($'000)	Objective										
	Outcome										
Manufacturing Costs ($'000)	Objective										
	Outcome										
Sales Commission ($'000)	Objective										
	Outcome										

PRODUCT MARKETING EXPENDITURES

Promotion ($'000)	Objective										
	Outcome										
Product Advertising ($'000)	Objective										
	Outcome										
Technical Support ($'000)	Objective										
	Outcome										
Licensing Costs ($'000)	Objective										
	Outcome										

UNALLOCATED MARKETING EXPENDITURES

Fixed Sales Force Costs ($'000)	Objective										
	Outcome										
Sales Force Training Costs ($'000)	Objective										
	Outcome										
Corporate Communication ($'000)	Objective										
	Outcome										
Research ($'000)	Objective										
	Outcome										
Development ($'000)	Objective										
	Outcome										
Market Research ($'000)	Objective										
	Outcome										
Total Marketing Expenditures ($'000)	Objective										
	Outcome										
Operational Contribution ($'000)	Objective										
	Outcome										
Licensing Revenues ($'000)	Objective										
	Outcome										

Net Marketing Contribution ($'000)	Objective										
	Outcome										
Others ($'000)	Objective										
	Outcome										

INDUSTRAT STRATEGIC PLANNING FORM

_____

_____

_____

_____

_____

_____

_____

_____

_____

_____

_____

_____

_____

_____

_____

_____

_____

_____

_____

_____

_____

_____

_____

_____

_____

FORECAST RESULTING FROM STRATEGIC PLANNING

Firm_____   Industry_____

GENERAL PERFORMANCE		1	2	3	4	5	6	7	8	9	10
Market Share (%) of $ Sales	Objective										
	Outcome										
Sales Revenue ($'000)	Objective										
	Outcome										
Manufacturing Costs ($'000)	Objective										
	Outcome										
Sales Commission ($'000)	Objective										
	Outcome										

PRODUCT MARKETING EXPENDITURES

		1	2	3	4	5	6	7	8	9	10
Promotion ($'000)	Objective										
	Outcome										
Product Advertising ($'000)	Objective										
	Outcome										
Technical Support ($'000)	Objective										
	Outcome										
Licensing Costs ($'000)	Objective										
	Outcome										

UNALLOCATED MARKETING EXPENDITURES

		1	2	3	4	5	6	7	8	9	10
Fixed Sales Force Costs ($'000)	Objective										
	Outcome										
Sales Force Training Costs ($'000)	Objective										
	Outcome										
Corporate Communication ($'000)	Objective										
	Outcome										
Research ($'000)	Objective										
	Outcome										
Development ($'000)	Objective										
	Outcome										
Market Research ($'000)	Objective										
	Outcome										
Total Marketing Expenditures ($'000)	Objective										
	Outcome										
Operational Contribution ($'000)	Objective										
	Outcome										
Licensing Revenues ($'000)	Objective										
	Outcome										

		1	2	3	4	5	6	7	8	9	10
Net Marketing Contribution ($'000)	Objective										
	Outcome										
Others ($'000)	Objective										
	Outcome										

INDUSTRAT STRATEGIC PLANNING FORM

_____

_____

_____

_____

_____

_____

_____

_____

_____

_____

_____

_____

_____

_____

_____

_____

_____

_____

_____

_____

_____

_____

_____

_____

_____

FORECAST RESULTING FROM STRATEGIC PLANNING

Firm_____   Industry_____

GENERAL PERFORMANCE		1	2	3	4	5	6	7	8	9	10
Market Share (%) of $ Sales	Objective										
	Outcome										
Sales Revenue ($'000)	Objective										
	Outcome										
Manufacturing Costs ($'000)	Objective										
	Outcome										
Sales Commission ($'000)	Objective										
	Outcome										

PRODUCT MARKETING EXPENDITURES

Promotion ($'000)	Objective										
	Outcome										
Product Advertising ($'000)	Objective										
	Outcome										
Technical Support ($'000)	Objective										
	Outcome										
Licensing Costs ($'000)	Objective										
	Outcome										

UNALLOCATED MARKETING EXPENDITURES

Fixed Sales Force Costs ($'000)	Objective										
	Outcome										
Sales Force Training Costs ($'000)	Objective										
	Outcome										
Corporate Communication ($'000)	Objective										
	Outcome										
Research ($'000)	Objective										
	Outcome										
Development ($'000)	Objective										
	Outcome										
Market Research ($'000)	Objective										
	Outcome										
Total Marketing Expenditures ($'000)	Objective										
	Outcome										
Operational Contribution ($'000)	Objective										
	Outcome										
Licensing Revenues ($'000)	Objective										
	Outcome										

Net Marketing Contribution ($'000)	Objective										
	Outcome										
Others ($'000)	Objective										
	Outcome										

INDUSTRAT STRATEGIC PLANNING FORM

_____

_____

_____

_____

_____

_____

_____

_____

_____

_____

_____

_____

_____

_____

_____

_____

_____

_____

_____

_____

_____

_____

_____

_____

_____

_____

_____

_____

FORECAST RESULTING FROM STRATEGIC PLANNING

Firm_____   Industry_____

GENERAL PERFORMANCE

		1	2	3	4	5	6	7	8	9	10
Market Share (%) of $ Sales	Objective										
	Outcome										
Sales Revenue ($'000)	Objective										
	Outcome										
Manufacturing Costs ($'000)	Objective										
	Outcome										
Sales Commission ($'000)	Objective										
	Outcome										

PRODUCT MARKETING EXPENDITURES

		1	2	3	4	5	6	7	8	9	10
Promotion ($'000)	Objective										
	Outcome										
Product Advertising ($'000)	Objective										
	Outcome										
Technical Support ($'000)	Objective										
	Outcome										
Licensing Costs ($'000)	Objective										
	Outcome										

UNALLOCATED MARKETING EXPENDITURES

		1	2	3	4	5	6	7	8	9	10
Fixed Sales Force Costs ($'000)	Objective										
	Outcome										
Sales Force Training Costs ($'000)	Objective										
	Outcome										
Corporate Communication ($'000)	Objective										
	Outcome										
Research ($'000)	Objective										
	Outcome										
Development ($'000)	Objective										
	Outcome										
Market Research ($'000)	Objective										
	Outcome										
Total Marketing Expenditures ($'000)	Objective										
	Outcome										
Operational Contribution ($'000)	Objective										
	Outcome										
Licensing Revenues ($'000)	Objective										
	Outcome										

		1	2	3	4	5	6	7	8	9	10
Net Marketing Contribution ($'000)	Objective										
	Outcome										
Others ($'000)	Objective										
	Outcome										

INDUSTRAT STRATEGIC PLANNING FORM

_____

_____

_____

_____

_____

_____

_____

_____

_____

_____

_____

_____

_____

_____

_____

_____

_____

_____

_____

_____

_____

_____

_____

_____

_____

_____

_____

_____

FORECAST RESULTING FROM STRATEGIC PLANNING

Firm_____   Industry_____

GENERAL PERFORMANCE		1	2	3	4	5	6	7	8	9	10
Market Share (%) of $ Sales	Objective										
	Outcome										
Sales Revenue ($'000)	Objective										
	Outcome										
Manufacturing Costs ($'000)	Objective										
	Outcome										
Sales Commission ($'000)	Objective										
	Outcome										

PRODUCT MARKETING EXPENDITURES

Promotion ($'000)	Objective										
	Outcome										
Product Advertising ($'000)	Objective										
	Outcome										
Technical Support ($'000)	Objective										
	Outcome										
Licensing Costs ($'000)	Objective										
	Outcome										

UNALLOCATED MARKETING EXPENDITURES

Fixed Sales Force Costs ($'000)	Objective										
	Outcome										
Sales Force Training Costs ($'000)	Objective										
	Outcome										
Corporate Communication ($'000)	Objective										
	Outcome										
Research ($'000)	Objective										
	Outcome										
Development ($'000)	Objective										
	Outcome										
Market Research ($'000)	Objective										
	Outcome										
Total Marketing Expenditures ($'000)	Objective										
	Outcome										
Operational Contribution ($'000)	Objective										
	Outcome										
Licensing Revenues ($'000)	Objective										
	Outcome										

Net Marketing Contribution ($'000)	Objective										
	Outcome										
Others ($'000)	Objective										
	Outcome										

INDUSTRAT STRATEGIC PLANNING FORM

FORECAST RESULTING FROM STRATEGIC PLANNING

Firm_____   Industry_____

GENERAL PERFORMANCE		1	2	3	4	5	6	7	8	9	10
Market Share (%) of $ Sales	Objective										
	Outcome										
Sales Revenue ($'000)	Objective										
	Outcome										
Manufacturing Costs ($'000)	Objective										
	Outcome										
Sales Commission ($'000)	Objective										
	Outcome										

PRODUCT MARKETING EXPENDITURES

Promotion ($'000)	Objective										
	Outcome										
Product Advertising ($'000)	Objective										
	Outcome										
Technical Support ($'000)	Objective										
	Outcome										
Licensing Costs ($'000)	Objective										
	Outcome										

UNALLOCATED MARKETING EXPENDITURES

Fixed Sales Force Costs ($'000)	Objective										
	Outcome										
Sales Force Training Costs ($'000)	Objective										
	Outcome										
Corporate Communication ($'000)	Objective										
	Outcome										
Research ($'000)	Objective										
	Outcome										
Development ($'000)	Objective										
	Outcome										
Market Research ($'000)	Objective										
	Outcome										
Total Marketing Expenditures ($'000)	Objective										
	Outcome										
Operational Contribution ($'000)	Objective										
	Outcome										
Licensing Revenues ($'000)	Objective										
	Outcome										

Net Marketing Contribution ($'000)	Objective										
	Outcome										
Others ($'000)	Objective										
	Outcome										

INDUSTRAT STRATEGIC PLANNING FORM

FORECAST RESULTING FROM STRATEGIC PLANNING

Firm_____   Industry_____

GENERAL PERFORMANCE

		1	2	3	4	5	6	7	8	9	10
Market Share (%) of $ Sales	Objective										
	Outcome										
Sales Revenue ($'000)	Objective										
	Outcome										
Manufacturing Costs ($'000)	Objective										
	Outcome										
Sales Commission ($'000)	Objective										
	Outcome										

PRODUCT MARKETING EXPENDITURES

Promotion ($'000)	Objective										
	Outcome										
Product Advertising ($'000)	Objective										
	Outcome										
Technical Support ($'000)	Objective										
	Outcome										
Licensing Costs ($'000)	Objective										
	Outcome										

UNALLOCATED MARKETING EXPENDITURES

Fixed Sales Force Costs ($'000)	Objective										
	Outcome										
Sales Force Training Costs ($'000)	Objective										
	Outcome										
Corporate Communication ($'000)	Objective										
	Outcome										
Research ($'000)	Objective										
	Outcome										
Development ($'000)	Objective										
	Outcome										
Market Research ($'000)	Objective										
	Outcome										
Total Marketing Expenditures ($'000)	Objective										
	Outcome										
Operational Contribution ($'000)	Objective										
	Outcome										
Licensing Revenues ($'000)	Objective										
	Outcome										

Net Marketing Contribution ($'000)	Objective										
	Outcome										
Others ($'000)	Objective										
	Outcome										

INDUSTRAT STRATEGIC PLANNING FORM

_____

_____

_____

_____

_____

_____

_____

_____

_____

_____

_____

_____

_____

_____

_____

_____

_____

_____

_____

_____

_____

_____

_____

_____

_____

FORECAST RESULTING FROM STRATEGIC PLANNING

Firm_____   Industry_____

GENERAL PERFORMANCE		1	2	3	4	5	6	7	8	9	10
Market Share (%) of $ Sales	Objective										
	Outcome										
Sales Revenue ($'000)	Objective										
	Outcome										
Manufacturing Costs ($'000)	Objective										
	Outcome										
Sales Commission ($'000)	Objective										
	Outcome										

PRODUCT MARKETING EXPENDITURES

Promotion ($'000)	Objective										
	Outcome										
Product Advertising ($'000)	Objective										
	Outcome										
Technical Support ($'000)	Objective										
	Outcome										
Licensing Costs ($'000)	Objective										
	Outcome										

UNALLOCATED MARKETING EXPENDITURES

Fixed Sales Force Costs ($'000)	Objective										
	Outcome										
Sales Force Training Costs ($'000)	Objective										
	Outcome										
Corporate Communication ($'000)	Objective										
	Outcome										
Research ($'000)	Objective										
	Outcome										
Development ($'000)	Objective										
	Outcome										
Market Research ($'000)	Objective										
	Outcome										
Total Marketing Expenditures ($'000)	Objective										
	Outcome										
Operational Contribution ($'000)	Objective										
	Outcome										
Licensing Revenues ($'000)	Objective										
	Outcome										

Net Marketing Contribution ($'000)	Objective										
	Outcome										
Others ($'000)	Objective										
	Outcome										

INDUSTRAT STRATEGIC PLANNING FORM

_____

_____

_____

_____

_____

_____

_____

_____

_____

_____

_____

_____

_____

_____

_____

_____

_____

_____

_____

_____

_____

_____

_____

_____

_____

_____

_____

FORECAST RESULTING FROM STRATEGIC PLANNING

Firm_____   Industry_____

GENERAL PERFORMANCE

		1	2	3	4	5	6	7	8	9	10
Market Share (%) of $ Sales	Objective										
	Outcome										
Sales Revenue ($'000)	Objective										
	Outcome										
Manufacturing Costs ($'000)	Objective										
	Outcome										
Sales Commission ($'000)	Objective										
	Outcome										

PRODUCT MARKETING EXPENDITURES

Promotion ($'000)	Objective										
	Outcome										
Product Advertising ($'000)	Objective										
	Outcome										
Technical Support ($'000)	Objective										
	Outcome										
Licensing Costs ($'000)	Objective										
	Outcome										

UNALLOCATED MARKETING EXPENDITURES

Fixed Sales Force Costs ($'000)	Objective										
	Outcome										
Sales Force Training Costs ($'000)	Objective										
	Outcome										
Corporate Communication ($'000)	Objective										
	Outcome										
Research ($'000)	Objective										
	Outcome										
Development ($'000)	Objective										
	Outcome										
Market Research ($'000)	Objective										
	Outcome										
Total Marketing Expenditures ($'000)	Objective										
	Outcome										
Operational Contribution ($'000)	Objective										
	Outcome										
Licensing Revenues ($'000)	Objective										
	Outcome										

Net Marketing Contribution ($'000)	Objective										
	Outcome										
Others ($'000)	Objective										
	Outcome										

INDUSTRAT STRATEGIC PLANNING FORM

_____

_____

_____

_____

_____

_____

_____

_____

_____

_____

_____

_____

_____

_____

_____

_____

_____

_____

_____

_____

_____

_____

FORECAST RESULTING FROM STRATEGIC PLANNING

Firm_____   Industry_____

GENERAL PERFORMANCE

		1	2	3	4	5	6	7	8	9	10
Market Share (%) of $ Sales	Objective										
	Outcome										
Sales Revenue ($'000)	Objective										
	Outcome										
Manufacturing Costs ($'000)	Objective										
	Outcome										
Sales Commission ($'000)	Objective										
	Outcome										

PRODUCT MARKETING EXPENDITURES

Promotion ($'000)	Objective										
	Outcome										
Product Advertising ($'000)	Objective										
	Outcome										
Technical Support ($'000)	Objective										
	Outcome										
Licensing Costs ($'000)	Objective										
	Outcome										

UNALLOCATED MARKETING EXPENDITURES

Fixed Sales Force Costs ($'000)	Objective										
	Outcome										
Sales Force Training Costs ($'000)	Objective										
	Outcome										
Corporate Communication ($'000)	Objective										
	Outcome										
Research ($'000)	Objective										
	Outcome										
Development ($'000)	Objective										
	Outcome										
Market Research ($'000)	Objective										
	Outcome										
Total Marketing Expenditures ($'000)	Objective										
	Outcome										
Operational Contribution ($'000)	Objective										
	Outcome										
Licensing Revenues ($'000)	Objective										
	Outcome										

Net Marketing Contribution ($'000)	Objective										
	Outcome										
Others ($'000)	Objective										
	Outcome										

Index